The COUNSELING SKILLS PRACTICE MANUAL

The COUNSELING SKILLS PRACTICE MANUAL

DAVID HUTCHINSON

Johnson State College, Vermont

SAGE

Los Angeles | London | New Delhi
Singapore | Washington DC

Los Angeles | London | New Delhi
Singapore | Washington DC

FOR INFORMATION:

SAGE Publications, Inc.
2455 Teller Road
Thousand Oaks, California 91320
E-mail: order@sagepub.com

SAGE Publications Ltd.
1 Oliver's Yard
55 City Road
London EC1Y 1SP
United Kingdom

SAGE Publications India Pvt. Ltd.
B 1/I 1 Mohan Cooperative Industrial Area
Mathura Road, New Delhi 110 044
India

SAGE Publications Asia-Pacific Pte. Ltd.
33 Pekin Street #02-01
Far East Square
Singapore 048763

Acquisitions Editor: Kassie Graves
Editorial Assistant: Courtney Munz
Production Editor: Astrid Virding
Typesetter: C&M Digitals (P) Ltd.
Proofreader: Dennis W. Webb
Cover Designer: Janet Kiesel
Marketing Manager: Katie Winter
Permissions Editor: Adele Hutchinson

Copyright © 2012 by SAGE Publications, Inc.

Printed in the United States of America

ISBN 978-1-4522-1687-4

This book is printed on acid-free paper.

11 12 13 14 15 10 9 8 7 6 5 4 3 2 1

Contents

Preface – A Note To Students

This Skills Practice Manual has been designed to accompany your text, *The Essential Counselor: Process, Skills, and Techniques* (2nd. ed.). It is meant to be a truly practical and helpful adjunct to the text and to the course that you are taking. There are 12 practice sessions in this manual, each of which includes opportunities to think about and practice a specific skill set.

These skill sessions were created to give you as much of a hands-on, real-world sense of what counseling work is like as possible. These are not academic exercises. Rather, they are preparation for the work that you will be doing shortly, either in field and internship experiences, or in a real counseling job. The more care and time you take with these, the better prepared you will be to do this work.

People who are new to this kind of work usually experience some anxiety. That's natural. When the door closes behind you and a new client, there is an uncertainty about what will happen next. The more practice you've had in simulated skills review sessions, the more comfortable you'll feel when people are really coming to you for help. Taking these practice sessions seriously will not only give you some additional tools for doing this work, but it will also help you feel more at ease as you begin to do it.

The practice sessions themselves can inherently foster some anxiety. It can be intimidating learning how to use these skills while being watched by other people. Some of these practice sessions may involve being watched, and the Lab Practice Model described in the text involves observation, as well. It would be weird not to feel at least a little anxiety in this kind of a setting. Live with it and accept it as a part of the learning process. You'll get used to being watched, to receiving feedback, and even to sometimes having recording equipment in the room.

You will come to see that you already have much of what is needed to work as a professional counselor. Your life experience, your interest in people, and your natural listening skills will serve you well. The intent of the text and this Skills Practice Manual is to help you supplement what you already have with an additional skill set. These skill sessions will also help you recognize the importance of your natural ability and experience, and will hopefully give you some added confidence about what you have to offer the people you see. If you already have some experience in the counseling field, these will be a helpful refresher.

A primary challenge for any new counselor has to do with being able to successfully manage her or his own anxiety—including worrying about being competent—while meeting a new client. Naturally, you will be concerned about doing a good job, but even that can be a distraction if it prevents you from hearing your client well. You will only be able to successfully observe and listen to your client to the degree that you can put your concerns about yourself aside. The practice sessions in this manual, as well as the other practice work you do in your coursework, will help you gain the confidence you need to not be overly distracted by concerns about yourself. They will also help you to decide about whether this really is the work you want to do.

The skills under review in this Skills Practice Manual are certainly not all you will need to be a proficient counselor. These are intended to provide you with some confidence and a foundation for being able to engage a new client. Other skills, some of which are described in *The Essential Counselor,* will also aid your work, as will your other coursework and your practical in-class and field experiences. The developmental model discussed in the text will help you apply the theory you learn to the actual work you do with clients.

The skills practice sessions outlined in this manual roughly follow the outline of the text, but not exactly. You may find that at some points your skills session under review for a given week is not exactly in synch with the text. If that is the case, you may want to read the relevant material in the text regarding that skill set before doing the practice sessions, even if the reading hasn't yet been assigned. This will better prepare you to think clearly about the skills you'll be practicing.

Be patient with yourself—and your student colleagues—as you work your way through these skills practice sessions. Allow yourself the right to make mistakes. As a ski instructor friend of mine says, "If you don't fall down occasionally, you're not trying."

Mostly, I hope that you find these skills practice sessions to be engaging and enjoyable. These are an introduction to the work of counseling, to work that is deeply satisfying. It is an honor and a privilege to work in such an intimate way with people, to hear their sorrows, their joys, their concerns. It is also a way of working where you learn a great deal about yourself as you learn about working with others. What a great side benefit. Not many other professions can make that claim.

I would welcome your feedback, your suggestions, and your questions.

David Hutchinson, PhD
Johnson State College

Johnson, Vermont
David.Hutchinson@jsc.edu

1

Getting Started

*Using Your Natural Interest
and Curiosity About People*

Introduction

You have been drawn to the helping professions because of some innate interest in how people behave, and also because of your natural inclination to do this kind of work. Perhaps you have been told you're a good listener, or you find yourself to be someone to whom people typically turn when there are problems. Maybe you grew up in a home where there were difficulties, and you learned how to "read" people as a strategy to keep things as safe as possible. It's possible that your life experiences have given you some very good intuitive skills that help you to see to the heart of the issues that people talk about, and you can respond in ways that are effective and even therapeutic.

All of these things taken together represent the best of what you'll be able to offer your clients. Your natural listening skills, your interest in what people have to say, and your cumulative life experience will serve as the foundation for how you will approach this work. They are the best things you have to offer your client.

The textbook that accompanies this manual, *The Essential Counselor,* presents many skills that you will be able to use in your work. Never lose sight of the fact, however, that it is your own self—you as a person—and your "wisdom" about life, that will drive the skills you use. Your basic assumptions about the nature of people and the theoretical ways you approach your work will help you in your work, as well.

Your course of study will undoubtedly state the importance of empathy as a single most important ingredient in the counseling process. Your ability to see the world through the eyes of another, to imagine with a high degree of accuracy what it would be like to be this other person, is what it means to be empathic. You will best be able to do this when you bring all of your life experience into the counseling space with you. The more of life you have experienced, the more you'll be able to accurately identify with your clients. This doesn't mean that you'll talk about these experiences of yours, but rather that these experiences will serve to help you understand what goes on for your client. This is why helping professionals who have a rich life history—including all of the good, bad, and ugly things that have been a part of their lives—are probably in the best position to provide this understanding.

The word "empathy" is closely related to the concept of "compassion." Both words have their root meanings in Latin words which roughly mean "suffering with another." This is what we do when we hear stories of abuse and trauma, of heartbreak and of loss . . . we suffer with another. Perhaps you will have some words of wisdom, or some suggestions that will help someone heal from the wounds she has endured, but the simple fact of your "suffering with" presence will, of itself, be primarily helpful.

Reflection Exercises: Your Natural Helping Foundation

The following set of reflection exercises is designed to help you articulate the experiences, the beliefs, the motivations, and natural skills you bring to this helping work.

The Reflection Exercises each begin with a set of questions. Try to be as honest with yourself as possible as you consider each of these. There are no right or wrong answers to these, rather they are meant to help you clearly articulate where you stand and what you think about some critical issues that will ultimately affect your work.

The first of these Reflection Exercises suggests that you do a brief life review. It will prompt you to look at the events and people who have influenced your decisions to become a counselor.

The second Reflection Exercise asks you to look at your underlying assumptions about the essential nature of people and what constitutes a healthy person. These assumptions, naturally, will impact how you approach the people you're counseling.

Finally, the last Reflection Exercise will ask you to review your natural helping skills, the set of personal characteristics and skills you think will benefit your work. You can, of course, also include in this review the things about which you have the most to learn.

When you have completed these reflection exercises and written about the influence of your life experience and beliefs on your future counseling work, you may be sharing this with one of your student peers or your instructor. You don't want to be writing about things that would unduly embarrass you. Perhaps you could write about those things in a language that only you would understand, or simply use euphemisms to describe particularly difficult experiences (e.g., "a tough time as a sophomore in high school").

REFLECTION EXERCISE #1: A LIFE REVIEW

Your cumulative life experience will be the greatest single asset you bring to your counseling work. The more varied, the richer your life experience, the greater will be your ability to understand the experiences of your clients. This does not mean you have to have had the same experiences they have had (they would never be exactly the same anyway), but the range and variety of experiences will simply expand your ability to understand. These experiences may provide the greatest motivation to do this work.

In a "bulleted" list fashion, name the significant people and events that you think have brought you to this place in time where you want to become a helping professional. Some of these may be positive influences, some may be less so. List as many as seem relevant and identify the positive (or otherwise) nature of the influence that this person/event has had on you.

- _____
- _____
- _____
- _____
- _____
- _____
- _____
- _____
- _____
- _____
- _____
- _____
- _____
- _____
- _____
- _____
- _____
- _____

REFLECTION EXERCISE #2: YOUR PERSONAL PHILOSOPHY AND CLOSELY HELD VALUES

Fundamental to your work with people will be your basic assumptions about the nature of people. Are we born flawed, or are we born as essentially "good?" What role does our upbringing have in shaping who we become? How does someone become psychologically healthy? What does it even mean to be "healthy," and should helping someone become healthy (whatever you think that means) be a goal of counseling?

Related to these basic assumptions, ask yourself about the primary values you hold that will shape your work with people? You might review the values outlined in the text as you review your own.

Take some time to contemplate these questions. There is a lot here. You might even want to think about what you've read—or consider reading—what others have said about these. These are critical philosophical questions which will have a huge impact on how you work with people, and it's best that you consider them at the outset of your career. Naturally, there probably will be some change in these as you mature in your development as a professional; yet some will maintain permanence.

When you have taken time to think about all this, perhaps making some notes in the process, compose a brief personal mission statement—your beliefs and values about life and helping others, if you want to call it something—that incorporates all of your thinking about these questions. This philosophy will intimately affect the counseling work you do. Again, you can present this here as a bulleted list.

- _____

- _____

- _____

- _____

- _____

- _____

- _____

- _____

- _____

- _____

- _____

- _____

- _____

- _____

- _____

REFLECTION EXERCISE #3: YOUR PERSONAL CHARACTERISTICS AND NATURAL SKILLS

You have a set of natural skills and personal characteristics that will serve as the backbone of your counseling work. Naturally, the skills you acquire and the theoretical approaches you learn about working with people will be important. They will be add-ons, however, to the critically central important role your own "person-hood" serves. Who you are as a person will intimately affect how you work with others.

In this third personal review, take some time to look at those skills and personal characteristics of yours that you think will most influence your work. Most of these will be positive assets and attributes, but you may identify some that are less than positive, things that you believe will need your attention and future work. The chapter in *The Essential Counselor* that talks about assessment and planning surveys the parts of a "whole person." You might want to take a look at this as you embark on this review of your own characteristics and skills.

After you've taken some time to think about these skills and characteristics, list them in the space that follows.

_____

_____

_____

_____

_____

_____

_____

_____

_____

_____

_____

_____

_____

_____

_____

Role Play: Using Your Natural Skills

The Essential Counselor outlines a lab practice model for role plays. In this model, there is a client, a counselor, and either one or two observers. You can review that model in the text and use it here, if it seems suitable. Alternatively, you could work with one other student, taking turns as counselor and client, or with a friend or relative, if another student is not available. If you are working with observers, their job is to remain silent during the role play, to keep time, and then to provide feedback at the end of the role play.

When you are in the client role (where another student or friend is being the counselor) you will talk about the reflections you've written about—your life experiences, your values and beliefs, and your natural helping skills—with the counselor. Talk about those things that feel safe. Do not feel compelled to share aspects of your life or beliefs that feel uncomfortable to talk about; those could be saved for discussion in your own personal counseling, not this skills training course.

Given that you most likely will not have time to discuss all that you've written, you can pick and choose to talk about those things that seem most relevant and best to talk about at this starting out point in this course. Take 20 minutes for this, and then spend 5 minutes talking with the person who served as your counselor about how this went. If there is an observer, that person can also share perspectives on the discussion.

Then the configuration shifts, where you switch roles, or where you rotate roles, if you've been working with one or two observers. When you are in the counseling role, you will want to do all you can to help your "client" talk about his/her life experiences, beliefs, and personal characteristics and natural skills. Use all of those natural skills you identified to help the other feel comfortable enough to talk and to draw him or her out.

Take time after each 20 minute role play to discuss it, particularly focusing on those things the counselor did that seemed to be most effective in moving the conversation along.

Remember that information that is shared in this, or any, role play should be held confidentially unless there is an explicit understanding that it is okay to talk about it with others. Naturally, if you are concerned about anyone's safety related to information that's been shared, you'll want to discuss that with your instructor. Safety trumps confidentiality.

When the role plays and discussion of them are completed, note some final comments and reflections in the space provided below. Then fill out the personal assessment question and comment section that follows. Finally, swap your assessment with a student colleague or give it to your instructor. This other person can add his thoughts to your assessment, and you may be reviewing his.

Comments About the Role Plays:

_____

_____

_____

_____

Concluding Personal Assessment: Personal Life Experiences, Beliefs, and Natural Skills and Characteristics

Name _____

Which of the following statements best reflects how clearly you have articulated your experiences, beliefs, and skills? Circle one:

1. I believe that I quite thoroughly understand my experiences, beliefs, and natural skills . . . and I know that I will be able to use them in my work with clients.

2. I understand these experiences, beliefs, and natural skills, but am not sure about how well I'll be able to use them in my counseling work.

3. I'm still pretty unclear about what my beliefs and skills are all about, and I'm not sure about how to use them.

Comments:

_____

_____

_____

_____

Concluding Peer and/or Instructor Assessment: Personal Life Experiences, Beliefs, and Natural Skills and Characteristics

Which of the following statements best reflects how clearly he/she has articulated his/her experiences, beliefs, and natural skills? Circle one:

1. I believe that he/she quite thoroughly understands his/her experiences, beliefs, and natural skills . . . and I know that he/she will be able to use them in his/her work with clients.

2. He/she understands these experiences and natural skills, but I am not sure about how well he/she will be able to use them in his/her counseling work.

3. He/she is still pretty unclear about what his/her beliefs and skills are all about, and I'm not sure how he/she will use them.

Reviewer Name _____

2

Giving and Receiving Feedback

Introduction

A critical aspect of developing your skills as a competent counselor involves learning how to give and receive feedback about what you're doing. You will want to give information to your student colleagues about how they're doing their counseling practicing, and you'll want to hear what they have to say about your developing skills, as well.

The expression, "giving feedback," means telling someone, quite specifically, what you've seen and heard her doing and your ideas about what she's done. This is like any supervisor telling someone about her work performance, and in counseling, supervision should always be available to help us determine what is effective in our work. Generally, the counseling supervisor will help you talk over your work with a specific client, perhaps brainstorming future courses of action and reflecting on those counselor actions that seem to be most helpful in moving things along. In this kind of counseling supervision, the supervisor is not acting in an evaluative role, but rather in a collaborative, mentoring fashion.

For our purposes, you will be primarily concerned with giving and receiving feedback with your student colleagues. You will serve as their counseling supervisor, they as yours. You will want to do this in a way that is mutually helpful and instructive. In order to be most effective, your way of giving information should use language that reflects your ideas in a way that you think the other will be able to receive the information without becoming defensive and guarded. The bottom line is that you want the person to whom you're giving feedback to be able to receive it and integrate it.

There are some general principles that will be helpful for you to know about as you begin to contemplate this whole business of learning how to give effective feedback.

Watch and
Listen Carefully

When you are serving in the observer/supervisor role, looking on as your colleagues are working on their counseling skills, watch and listen closely as the counselor interacts with her client. This may seem obvious, but this is a different kind of observing and listening than you may be used to. These are not casual, social conversations. You will want to catch every counselor intervention (the things the counselor says) and note the impact on her client. Does the interaction following these interventions become more personal and important, or do things shift away in irrelevant or less important directions?

Watch the nonverbal behaviors of both the counselor and client. Is the counselor use of nonverbal behavior promoting intimacy and open communication, or do the nonverbal behaviors—facial expressions, voice tone, eye contact, body posture—suggest inattention and distraction, or guardedness and protection?

Everything the counselor you are observing does and says is important. You will want to take it all in, maybe even making some written notes about what you observe, and then prepare yourself to share what you've seen and heard.

Share What You've Observed: Keep It Short and Simple, and Keep It Behavioral

When a counseling session is over and your observation is complete, you'll want to share what you've seen and heard. You will most likely be really interested in the things the client has been talking about, and you may be tempted to share your perspectives about the issues that have been discussed. While there may be time, at some point, to do that, remember that your primary responsibility in these learning situations is to provide feedback to the counselor about skills development.

Share what you've seen and heard with the counselor, sticking to directly observable behaviors, the actual things that were done or said. Be as concrete as possible. Talk about what you saw and heard, and about your ideas related to the impact those things said and done had on the client. Do what you can to be non-evaluative, nonjudgmental. Try to avoid words like "good" and "bad" when giving feedback, for those imply judgment. Focus on those counselor behaviors, verbal and nonverbal, that seemed to have the most significant impact on the client.

Support, Support, Support

Always bear in mind that your feedback is designed to assist your colleague in doing a better job, to improve her skills. The primary focus of this counseling skills practice is not on resolving client issues, rather on counseling skill development. It is certainly not your job to be critical or punitive. Your feedback will best be heard and truly taken to heart when it is perceived to be coming from a place of positive support. Try to find ways to be encouraging.

People learn best when they feel safe, but when there is an edge of anxiety. The learning situation itself, the observed counseling session, typically carries ample anxiety, so whatever you do to be supportive will help create an optimal learning environment. Your feedback, then, will be given without evaluation. It will simply state the facts, what you saw and heard happening. "When you said this and this," for example, "this is how your client responded."

Sharing Your Thoughts and Feelings About What You've Seen and Heard

It is possible, and sometimes helpful, to add your thoughts – including your feelings – about something the counselor has done. You might share your observations about something the counselor said, and then take a stab at guessing why the counselor said what she did. This should be done tentatively, in a spirit of mutual inquiry. Similarly, you can share your feelings (sad, mad, glad, scared, etc.), as if you had been on the receiving end of what the counselor has done . . . as if you had been the client, in other words.

Supervision and Counseling as Parallel Paths

Much of what you will do in your role as observer/supervisor is exactly like what you will do in your role as counselor. As a counselor, you want your client to feel understood, respected, and valued. This is exactly what you want the counselor to experience when you are supervising her. Empathy is a key ingredient in counseling relationships – so, too, in effective supervisory relationships. The more that you can experience the therapeutic world through your counselor's eyes, the more productive your supervision will be.

Just as the counselor is striving to achieve a working alliance with her client, you are also trying to build a supervisory alliance with your counselor. Where there is trust, when you are experienced as truly being invested in the counselor doing well, good things can happen.

Example: Giving Constructive Feedback

Consider the following situation. Your student colleague is playing the role of a school counselor. She has the following interchange with your student colleague who is in the role of the parent of a high school age boy:

Client: I don't know what to do. My boy wants to drop out of school. He's only 16, and he wants to drop out. His teachers give him a terrible time. Nobody here cuts him any slack. I just don't know what to do.

Counselor: Maybe you could just review with him all the reasons he should stay in school. I know that you know dropping out is a bad idea.

Client: Well, yeah, sure. I know that dropping out is a bad idea. But I don't know how to convince him. He's stubborn.

Counselor: You're his mother. I'm sure he'll listen to you.

Client: Are you kidding?! Do you have any kids?

As a supervisor, how would you give the counselor some feedback about this interchange? Following are three possible alternatives.

Feedback Option #1: "When you told your client that she should just be able to tell her son to stay in school, she seemed to get pretty defensive."

Feedback Option #2: "Your first comment, about the mom reviewing the reasons her son should stay in school . . . . I'm not sure it accurately reflected the gist of what she was saying. It sounded like you had some definite ideas about what she should do."

Feedback Option #3: "I heard you trying to be encouraging, giving your client some advice about what to do. I assume you were trying to support her, but I got a little nervous about the possibilities for you getting into a power tussle with her."

Which of these options seems most appealing to you? Why?

_____

_____

_____

If you don't care for any of the above feedback messages, what might you say to this counselor? Create your own feedback message here:

_____

_____

_____

Example 2: Giving Constructive Feedback

Here's another situation. One of your student colleagues is role playing a client who is unhappy with his job. The student who is acting as the counselor is trying to find out more about this unhappiness, and is trying to help his client explore other options.

Client: I never wanted to sell insurance. My father sold insurance his whole life, and he finally just retired. I don't think he liked what he did either, but he was the one who convinced me all those years ago that it was a good way to make an honest living.

Counselor: So how many years have you been doing this?

Client: 15. 15 long, long years.

Counselor: Yeah, I can tell that you really don't enjoy this work. And you're worried about there being another 15.

Client: You bet. I sure don't want to go through my life just waiting to retire, like my Dad. I can't imagine anything worse. I mean, I spend most of my waking hours working, and I'd like to spend that time doing something I look forward to. I wake up in the morning now and say, "I can't believe I have to go that office again." It's awful.

Counselor: You've seen the future – particularly with your Dad's situation – and it's not pretty. You're really fed up.

Again, as the supervisor, how would you give feedback to the counselor about this interchange? Here are three possible alternatives to consider:

Feedback Option #1: I noticed that when you asked that first question you got a really clipped, short answer. And then when you reflected more on what this guy said about his work and his job, he really seemed to get into it.

Feedback Option #2: This last thing you said . . . about seeing the future. You've put your client's unhappiness with his work in a different language, put a new twist on it, and I bet he'll be able to run with this.

Feedback Option #3: The things you said to your client, the ways you reworded what he'd said, seemed pretty congruent with what he meant . . . at least he responded that way. And you really seemed to be in synch with his frustration, too. If I were your client, I'd really appreciate this.

Which of these options seems most appealing to you? Why?

_____

_____

_____

If you don't care for any of the above feedback messages, what might you say to this counselor? Create your own feedback message here:

_____

_____

_____

Receiving Feedback

Naturally, when you are working as a counselor – either in practice sessions or professionally – you will be receiving feedback from a supervisor. Some of this supervisory feedback may be from peers, some from instructors, some from supervisors on the job. The following guidelines may prove helpful for you in being on the receiving end of feedback, regardless of the work/study situation:

- Paraphrase what was said so that your supervisor knows that you've accurately heard what's been said.
- Try to be non-defensive when receiving feedback. You don't have to necessarily agree with everything that's being given to you, but you can at least sit with it for a while to see how much of what's been observed or suggested might be accurate. Remember, this is simply one other person's perspective on what has transpired.

- Accept what seems to fit, reject what seems to be off the mark. This will be easier to do the more experience you have, because you'll have a better sense of whether a specific piece of feedback seems congruent with other information you've received.

DVD Observation of Giving and Receiving Feedback

Watch any one of the counseling sessions on the DVD that accompanies *The Essential Counselor*. Make some notes and think about what kinds of feedback, and questions, you might have for the counselor. Then watch the review/feedback session that follows the counseling session. Then respond to the following:

1. Did the feedback session that you viewed seem to generally hold to the suggestions that have been made in this chapter about giving and receiving constructive feedback? Was it specific, non-evaluative, and supportive?

_____

_____

_____

2. What would you have added – or asked about – if you had been present at this review session?

_____

_____

_____

3. Create one-two pieces of feedback that you might share with the counselor in response to the counseling session that you just watched.

_____

_____

_____

4. Did the counselor in the DVD feedback/review session seem to receive the feedback in a constructive fashion? Discuss.

_____

_____

_____

When you have finished reflecting on these questions, fill out the personal assessment question and comment section that follows. Finally, swap your assessments with a student colleague or give it to your instructor. This other person can add their thoughts to your assessment, and you may be reviewing theirs.

Concluding Personal Assessment: Giving and Receiving Feedback

Name _____

Which of the following statements best reflects how well you think you understand and will be able to accurately utilize these skills? Circle one:

1. I believe that I quite thoroughly understand these skills, and I know that I will be able to use them in my work with clients.

2. I understand these skills, but am not sure about how well I'll be able to use them in my counseling work.

3. I'm still pretty unclear about what these skills are all about, and I'm not sure about how to use them.

Comments:

_____

_____

_____

_____

Concluding Peer and/or Instructor Assessment: Giving and Receiving Feedback

Which of the following statements best reflects how well you think this person understands and will be able to accurately utilize these skills? Circle one:

1. I believe that this person clearly understands these skills, and I am confident that he/she will be able to use them in his/her work with clients.

2. These skills are understood, but am not sure about how well he/she will be able to use them in his/her counseling work.

3. He/she is still pretty unclear about these skills and their use.

Comments:

_____

_____

_____

_____

Reviewer Name _____

3

Getting Started With a New Client

Nonverbal Behavior

Introduction

Your beginnings with a new client will involve a great deal of talking. You will ask questions and use a number of other verbal skills to engage this person and to find out more about what has prompted him to seek counseling. Counseling is a particularly verbal-oriented activity, and much of this course focuses on the different verbal interactions that can help or hinder client growth.

In addition to these verbal interactions, however—the things you and your client say to each other—there are also the obvious and more subtle nonverbal interactions that will have significant impact on the development of the relationship between the two of you.

As a counselor, you will be interested in observing your client's nonverbal behavior. You will, for example, want to watch how he carries himself, how comfortable he seems to be in his body, how he dresses, how he talks, and the ways he engages you with his eyes. You are interested in all of these behaviors, and more—in addition to all of the verbal things that he tells you—that provide information about this person with whom you're sitting.

You will also be interested in learning more about your own nonverbal behavior, all of the ways you behave that will influence how your client begins to interact with you. You are certainly interested in utilizing those nonverbal behaviors that invite your client to talk more personally with you.

**DVD
Observation of
Nonverbal
Behavior**

Watch the session entitled, "Cultural Issues in Counseling With an Adolescent Client," on the DVD that accompanies *The Essential Counselor*. In this session, the counselor, Anne, is trying to engage Jane, who is role playing the young woman client who is having difficulty in school. Also watch the follow-up review/feedback session that follows this session.

Take note of the nonverbal behavior of both the client and counselor. Respond to the following:

1. What, specifically, about the client's nonverbal behavior communicates how she is feeling?

   _____

   _____

   _____

2. Does the client's nonverbal behavior change over the course of the session?

   _____

   _____

   _____

3. What counselor nonverbal behaviors do you think play a role in communication in this session? And are they useful in promoting communication?

   _____

   _____

   _____

4. In the review session, some comments are made about the use of nonverbal behavior, including seating positioning. Do you agree with these comments?

   _____

   _____

   _____

Role Play Exercises: Communicating Feelings Nonverbally

There are some reflection and observation exercises in the text, *The Essential Counselor,* that will help you become more aware of your clients' nonverbal behavior, as well as your own. The following role play exercises will help you to become even more conscious of the ways nonverbal behavior influences others. They are designed to help you become more aware of the nonverbal behavior of others, as well as of the role your own nonverbal behavior has in communicating what you feel to another. These exercises are designed to heighten your awareness of the specific impact of facial expression, body language (including posture and position, and the use of your hands), and eye contact on communication. Finally, there will be an opportunity for you to reflect on your voice tone as an influencing factor in communication with another.

First, find another person with whom to do these exercises. It would be best if this is someone who is studying this material with you, but a friend or relative will suffice. If it is not possible to do this with another person, you can modify it by using a mirror and practicing these behaviors yourself.

It would be great if you have access to video equipment and can find someone to video this. It would be very helpful for you to watch your own behavior when you've completed the exercises.

Role Play: Facial Expression

Take turns with each other communicating *sadness*—without words, using only facial expression. Thirty seconds for each of you should suffice. Then take a minute or two to share your observations with each other. After you've talked with each other about your observation, make a few written notes about these observations here.

I observed in the other:

_____

_____

_____

I observed in myself:

_____

_____

_____

I would rate my ability to express sadness facially as (circle the appropriate number):

1. I didn't have a clue about how to do this. I might even have communicated another emotion.

2. Minimally effective. Lots of room for more expressiveness.

3. Very expressive. Accurate portrayal of feeling.

Now take turns with each other communicating *anger*—without words, using only facial expression. Thirty seconds for each of you to do this should be sufficient. Then take a minute or two to share your observations with each other. After you've talked with each other about your observation, make a few written notes about these observations here.

I observed in the other:

_____

_____

_____

I observed in myself:

_____

_____

_____

I would rate my ability to express anger facially as (circle the appropriate number):

1. I didn't have a clue about how to do this. I might even have communicated another emotion.
2. Minimally effective. Lots of room for more expressiveness.
3. Very expressive. Accurate portrayal of feeling.

Next, take turns with each other communicating *joy*—without words, using only facial expression. Thirty seconds for each of you to do this should be sufficient. Then take a minute or two to share your observations with each other. After you've talked with each other about your observation, make a few written notes about these observations here.

I observed in the other:

_____

_____

_____

I observed in myself:

_____

_____

_____

I would rate my ability to express joy facially as (circle the appropriate number):

1. I didn't have a clue about how to do this. I might even have communicated another emotion.

2. Minimally effective. Lots of room for more expressiveness.

3. Very expressive. Accurate portrayal of feeling.

Role Play: Body Language

Take turns with each other communicating *sadness*—without words, using only your body language—including your posture, your hand gestures, your sitting position—as you sit with your partner. Thirty seconds for each of you to do this should be sufficient. Then take a minute or two to share your observations with each other. After you've talked with each other about your observation, make a few written notes about these observations here.

I observed in the other:

_____

_____

_____

I observed in myself:

_____

_____

_____

I would rate my ability to express sadness with my body as (circle the appropriate number):

1. I didn't have a clue about how to do this. I might even have communicated another emotion.

2. Minimally effective. Lots of room for more expressiveness.

3. Very expressive. Accurate portrayal of feeling.

Now take turns with each other communicating *anger*—without words, using only body language. Thirty seconds for each of you to do this should be sufficient. Then take a minute or two to share your observations with each other. After you've talked with each other about your observation, make a few written notes about these observations here.

I observed in the other:

_____

_____

_____

I observed in myself:

_____

_____

_____

I would rate my ability to express anger with my body as (circle the appropriate number):

1. I didn't have a clue about how to do this. I might even have communicated another emotion.

2. Minimally effective. Lots of room for more expressiveness.

3. Very expressive. Accurate portrayal of feeling.

Next, take turns with each other communicating *joy*—without words, using only body language. Thirty seconds for each of you to do this should be sufficient. Then take a minute or two to share your observations with each other. After you've talked with each other about your observation, make a few written notes about these observations here.

I observed in the other:

_____

_____

_____

I observed in myself:

_____

_____

_____

I would rate my ability to express joy with my body as (circle the appropriate number):

1. I didn't have a clue about how to do this. I might even have communicated another emotion.

2. Minimally effective. Lots of room for more expressiveness.

3. Very expressive. Accurate portrayal of feeling.

Role Play: Eye Contact and Voice Tone

This exercise allows you to talk, and to listen, as well as to observe the function eye contact and voice tone have on communication. First, think about the place, or places, where you grew up. Then have a 10-minute, or so, conversation with your partner about these places. This is an informal conversation where you can take turns sharing information. When the 10 minutes are up, take a couple of minutes to first discuss how eye contact affected the discussion. How much did you, as well as your partner, maintain eye contact . . . and how much did you look away? Were there any times when ongoing eye contact became uncomfortable? Why?

Then take a little more time to write some notes about your observations.

I observed in the other:

_____

_____

_____

I observed in myself:

_____

_____

_____

I would rate my ability to maintain appropriate eye contact as (circle one number):

1. Not great. I have trouble maintaining eye contact, sometimes when I'm speaking, sometimes when listening.

2. Not bad. I find myself letting my eyes wander sometimes.

3. I have no trouble maintaining solid eye contact, and I don't overdo it—I know when to look away occasionally, so that I don't appear overly intrusive, or to be staring.

Now take some time to reflect, similarly, about your (and your partner's) voice tone in this exercise. Talk with each other about how voice tone—loudness, softness, clarity, etc.—affected the conversation. And, finally, make note here of your observations.

I observed in the other:

_____

_____

_____

I observed in myself:

_____

_____

_____

I would rate my ability to use voice tone in a way that is helpful in communicating with someone as (circle one number):

1. Not great. I have trouble with this (either sounding too loud, or too soft, too tentative). Explain:

   _____

   _____

   _____

2. Not bad.

3. No problems. I am able to speak clearly and confidently when I am talking about myself, and my voice tone is appropriately inviting when I am drawing someone into conversation.

When the role plays and discussion of them are completed, note some final comments and reflection in the space provided below. Then fill out the personal assessment question and comment section that follows. Finally, swap your assessment with a student colleague or give it to your instructor. This other person can add her thoughts to your assessment, and you may be reviewing hers.

Concluding Role Play Comments:

_____

_____

_____

_____

Concluding Personal Assessment: Observing and Using Nonverbal Behaviors

Name _____

Which of the following statements best reflects how well you think you understand and will be able to accurately utilize these skills? Circle one:

1. I believe that I quite thoroughly understand these skills, and I know that I will be able to use them in my work with clients.

2. I understand these skills, but am not sure about how well I'll be able to use them in my counseling work.

3. I'm still pretty unclear about what these skills are all about, and I'm not sure about how to use them.

Comments:

_____

_____

_____

_____

Concluding Peer and/or Instructor Assessment: Observing and Using Nonverbal Behaviors

Which of the following statements best reflects how well you think this person understands and will be able to accurately utilize these skills? Circle one:

1. I believe that this person clearly understands these skills, and I am confident that he/she will be able to use them in his/her work with clients.

2. These skills are understood, but am not sure about how well he/she will be able to use them in his/her counseling work.

3. He/she is still pretty unclear about these skills and their use.

Comments:

_____

_____

_____

_____

Reviewer Name _____

4

Using Questions to Engage and Fact-Find

Introduction

You will need to ask questions to find out why your client has come for counseling, and also to find out about her, about her background, and about her current situation. The setting in which you work will determine a good deal about what kinds of information you'll need to retrieve from your new client. Generally, regardless of your work setting, you will want to get an idea about who she is and about what she wants out of counseling.

The ways in which you use these questions will also, in addition to gathering information, play a role in engaging her. Your effective use of questions will assist your greater counseling effort, particularly in helping you to develop the all-important relationship between the two of you—the effective therapeutic alliance.

Good questions thus serve the double role of eliciting information and creating connection between the two of you. Good questions are intelligent and relevant to the task at hand. They don't ask for unnecessary information. If you are asking a series of questions, they ideally build on each other, following a train of thought, not shifting topics. Take the following example:

> A young mother has come to you because her infant son is very fussy, seems inconsolable, and she's at her wit's end about how to deal with this. The child's continual crying is driving her frantic. This is her first visit with you.

What questions might you ask her that will help you find out about and clarify her situation, while at the same time show her that you're concerned and willing to help her find some relief? Your work setting might have some specific things you need to find out as part of its intake procedures, but beyond that you probably have the latitude to ask questions of your own. Any of the following questions might serve to get things rolling:

> How long has this been going on?
>
> What kinds of help and support do you have in dealing with this?
>
> Have you had your baby checked out by a doctor, to make sure nothing's physically wrong?

How have you tried to comfort him?

Do you have other children?

All of these questions seem relevant. While some require briefer responses than others, each is an invitation to talk more about this difficult situation.

You will try to avoid asking questions which seem immediately irrelevant, or even foolish, like:

What color hair does he have?

Have you gotten him any new clothes?

Were you an only child?

The first two questions here are unnecessary and have nothing to do with the mom's dilemma. The third, while perhaps being interesting later on to examine the ways in which how she was parented affect how she is parenting, is inappropriate here. The specifics of the immediate situation need to be explored first.

Note that some questions require very little in the way of response. These questions, which are referred to as *fact-finding* questions, can typically be answered with a one or two word response. Examples of these kinds of questions include, *How old are you? Where do you live? Where do you work?* While each question may elicit some piece of information you're looking for, they can begin to sound like an interrogation when too many are strung together. Before asking any of these kinds of questions, you can always ask yourself if this is a piece of information you really need to know, and if so, are there other ways to go to patiently seek it out (we'll explore some of those "other ways" in later chapters). Asking lots of these kinds of questions also makes you work harder, with less of the responsibility going to the client for generating material. When you think you're working too hard, you probably are.

The other kind of question is designed to let the client elaborate and pursue a response with more depth. This kind of question is referred to as an *engagement question*. The term "engagement" is used because, in addition to gathering information, these questions also serve to help connect you to your client. It shows her that you are willing to give her a lot of room to tell you about her situation, and in the way she wants to tell it. It allows her to control the flow of information and the pace by which she shares it with you.

When we consider the case of the mom with the crying child, examples of *engagement questions* might include, from the ones already posed:

How have you tried to comfort him?

What kinds of help and support do you have in dealing with this?

Each of these questions might allow her to begin to tell her story about her trials and tribulations as a young mom, and about the specifics of this difficult situation.

EXERCISE: USING QUESTIONS

What other kinds of things might you want to know about this woman's difficult situation, and how could you ask questions to best find out about these? In the following space, first list three specific, *fact-finding* questions you might pose to her:

1.

    Circle one of the following numbers.

    1. This question is relevant and important.   2. I don't really need to know this.   3. I have no idea why I asked this.

2.

    Circle one of the following numbers.

    1. This question is relevant and important.   2. I don't really need to know this.   3. I have no idea why I asked this.

3.

    Circle one of the following numbers.

    1. This question is relevant and important.   2. I don't really need to know this.   3. I have no idea why I asked this.

Now try your hand at asking three *engagement questions* of the same client.

4.

    Circle one of the following numbers.

    1. This question is relevant and important.   2. I don't really need to know this.   3. I have no idea why I asked this.

5.

    Circle one of the following numbers.

    1. This question is relevant and important.   2. I don't really need to know this.   3. I have no idea why I asked this.

6.

    Circle one of the following numbers.

    1. This question is relevant and important.   2. I don't really need to know this.   3. I have no idea why I asked this.

Now here's another example:

You are sitting in your school counseling office with a 16-year-old who was caught shop-lifting last night. He was released into the custody of his parents who have asked that he come in to see you this morning. He's a new student in your school and you've only met him briefly on one former occasion.

What kinds of things might you want to know about this young man and about his situation, and how could you ask questions to best find out about these? In the following space, first list three specific, *fact-finding* questions you might pose:

1.

   Circle one of the following numbers.

   1. This question is relevant and important.   2. I don't really need to know this.   3. I have no idea why I asked this.

2.

   Circle one of the following numbers.

   1. This question is relevant and important.   2. I don't really need to know this.   3. I have no idea why I asked this.

3.

   Circle one of the following numbers.

   1. This question is relevant and important.   2. I don't really need to know this.   3. I have no idea why I asked this.

Now try your hand at asking three *engagement* questions of the same student.

4.

   Circle one of the following numbers.

   1. This question is relevant and important.   2. I don't really need to know this.   3. I have no idea why I asked this.

5.

   Circle one of the following numbers.

   1. This question is relevant and important.   2. I don't really need to know this.   3. I have no idea why I asked this.

6.

   Circle one of the following numbers.

   1. This question is relevant and important.   2. I don't really need to know this.   3. I have no idea why I asked this.

And, finally, a third example.

You have a new client who has been referred to you by a work supervisor at a local software development company. This young man has been missing work and is not as productive recently as he has been. The supervisor suspects that there are problems at home, and he wants this man to get help so his job performance will improve. If the performance doesn't improve, your client might lose his job.

What kinds of things might you want to know about this young man and about his situation, and how could you ask questions to best find out about these? In the following space, first list three specific, *fact-finding* questions you might pose:

1.

   Circle one of the following numbers.

   1. This question is relevant and important.   2. I don't really need to know this.   3. I have no idea why I asked this.

2.

   Circle one of the following numbers.

   1. This question is relevant and important.   2. I don't really need to know this.   3. I have no idea why I asked this.

3.

   Circle one of the following numbers.

   1. This question is relevant and important. 2. I don't really need to know this.   3. I have no idea why I asked this.

Now try your hand at asking three *engagement* questions of the same client.

4.

   Circle one of the following numbers.

   1. This question is relevant and important.   2. I don't really need to know this.   3. I have no idea why I asked this.

5.

   Circle one of the following numbers.

   1. This question is relevant and important.   2. I don't really need to know this.   3. I have no idea why I asked this.

6.

   Circle one of the following numbers.

   1. This question is relevant and important.   2. I don't really need to know this.   3. I have no idea why I asked this.

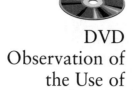

DVD Observation of the Use of Questions

On the DVD of role plays that accompanies *The Essential Counselor,* watch the role play entitled, 'Cultural Issues in Working With an Adolescent Client." In this role play, Jane is acting as an adolescent having some difficulties at her new high school. Anne is serving as her counselor, trying to find out the specifics of what is happening and also trying to make a connection with this young woman. In particular, listen to the questions Anne asks, perhaps making notes as the interview unfolds, and then respond to the following:

1. Were the questions Anne asked primarily of the fact-finding or engagement variety? Give an example or two of each kind that Anne asked.

_____

_____

_____

2. How effective were the questions Anne asked? What might you have done differently?

_____

_____

_____

3. It's interesting that a primary issue in this counseling session had to do with the client's discomfort with questions that people in her school were asking her. What was this about, and what implications would this have for the counselor? And how did you think Anne handled this?

_____

_____

_____

Role Play Exercise: Using Questions

Find someone with whom you can do this exercise, ideally someone from your class, but a friend or relative can work, as well.

Have your partner take 5 minutes to describe his current living space . . . apartment, condo, house, whatever. Your job in listening to your partner will be to ask only fact-finding and engagement questions . . . only questions. At the end of the 5-minute interview take some time to talk about the kinds of questions you asked. It would be best if you can tape-record the interview so you can go back to hear each question you asked. Do whatever you can to recall each of these questions, and then reflect on your proficiency with this skill in the space below. Talk about what was going on for you as you formulated questions, about how relatively important/relevant each question seemed to be, and what kind of response was elicited from your partner after it was asked. Then, if you are working with another student, switch roles and do it again.

When the role plays and discussion of them are completed, note some final comments and reflections in the space provided below. Then fill out the personal assessment question and comment section that follows. Finally, swap your assessments with a student colleague or give it to your instructor. This other person can add his thoughts to your assessment, and you may be reviewing his.

Comments About the Role Play:

_____

_____

_____

_____

Concluding Personal Assessment: Using Questions

Name _____

Which of the following statements best reflects how well you think you understand and will be able to accurately utilize these skills? Circle one:

1. I believe that I quite thoroughly understand these skills, and I know that I will be able to use them in my work with clients.

2. I understand these skills, but am not sure about how well I'll be able to use them in my counseling work.

3. I'm still pretty unclear about what these skills are all about, and I'm not sure about how to use them.

Comments:

_____

_____

_____

_____

Concluding Peer and/or Instructor Assessment: Using Questions

Which of the following statements best reflects how well you think this person understands and will be able to accurately utilize these skills? Circle one:

1. I believe that this person clearly understands these skills, and I am confident that he/she will be able to use them in his/her work with clients.

2. These skills are understood, but am not sure about how well he/she will be able to use them in his/her counseling work.

3. He/she is still pretty unclear about these skills and their use.

Comments:

_____

_____

_____

_____

Reviewer Name _____

5

Using Reflections for Engagement and for the Exploration of Feeling

Introduction

You can best communicate your capacity for listening to and understanding who your client is by accurately responding to what he says. It is through this accurate responding that you will best convey your desire for empathic connection to him . . . your ability to see and comprehend the world as he does. Because being able to make accurate *reflections* is such an important counseling skill, perhaps the most important of all the skills you'll have at your disposal, this is the longest chapter of this skills practice manual. The intent is to give you a significant opportunity to practice this important skill. It is through your accurate listening and responding that your client will feel understood, and in this understanding will begin to reveal himself more deeply.

You have seen how the skillful use of questions can help to begin to form the foundation for the development of an alliance with your client. Your intelligent and respectful inquiry with these questions will demonstrate your capacity to grasp what your client is bringing you.

Accurately *reflecting* what he says, in addition to those intelligent questions you've asked, will contribute significantly to your being seen as trustworthy. Truly grasping the content of what has been said, and then thoughtfully giving it back in a way that is a little different, in a way that has your own "spin" on it, will let your client move more deeply into the material. This kind of reflection is not just a restatement or re-ordering of the words that your client has said—that would more be like simply parroting—but is rather a thoughtful reworking of the material in your own language and in a way that keeps the accurate meaning of what your client has said.

Reflection Examples

Consider the following: A man is sitting in your office talking about his daughter's upcoming wedding. He is not sure the man she's marrying is right for her. He says,

"I just don't trust the guy. There's something about him that makes me nervous, like he's not going to be good to her. I don't like the way he looks at other women, and he's just a little too slick for comfort."

Here are some alternative *reflections* that you might make:

1. You're having a hard time backing your daughter's choice of a mate.

2. For some reason, this guy just doesn't seem like a good pick.

3. It's tough to warm up to a man . . . especially one who wants to marry your daughter . . . who's got a roving eye.

What do you like, or not like, about each of these? Could you see yourself saying one of these? Do the reflections seem accurate, and could they help to move the conversation along meaningfully? If not, think about alternatives that you might use.

Alternative 1.

_____

_____

_____

Alternative 2.

_____

_____

_____

Here's another situation: A woman about to be married is telling you about her overbearing father. She says, "He's so controlling. Ever since I've been a little girl he's figured that it's his job to run my life. He thinks I'm incapable of making decent decisions. He doesn't even think I'm marrying the right guy."

Here are some alternative *reflections* you might make here:

1. You're sick of being treated like a baby.

2. You can't believe that your Dad can't even let you get married without somehow implying that you're doing it wrong.

3. A whole lifetime of being judged and second-guessed.

What do you like, or not like, about each of these? Could you see yourself saying one of these? Do the reflections seem accurate, and could they help to move the conversation along meaningfully? If not, think about alternatives that you might use.

Alternative 1.

_____

_____

_____

Alternative 2.

_____

_____

_____

Finally, here's a third situation. A man is talking with you about his impending wedding. He's marrying a young woman he really loves, but he's troubled about the relationship she has with her father. He says, "You know, she's wonderful, absolutely wonderful. But she's got this thing going on with her father that scares me. She thinks he's trying to control her, he treats her like a kid, and I wonder what all this is going to be like after we're married."

Here are some alternative *reflections* you might make here:

1. You really love this woman, but there's this whole package that comes with her.

2. There's this really complicated thing between the two of them, and you wonder how you'll fit into it.

3. Getting married is getting complicated.

What do you like, or not like, about each of these? Could you see yourself saying one of these? Do the reflections seem accurate, and could they help to move the conversation along meaningfully? If not, think about alternatives that you might use.

Alternative 1.

_____

_____

_____

Alternative 2.

_____

_____

_____

EXERCISE: CREATING AND RATING YOUR REFLECTIONS

Following are a number of examples of things your new clients might be saying to you. With each of them, pose three alternative *reflections*. Rate each of your *reflections,* as follows: +1 (accurate and additive); 0 (neutral, does not distort, does not add); or −1 (distorts and detracts):

1. "You know, I've pretty much had it with my job. It's gotten so routine I'm bored out of my head. If it wasn't for the paycheck and the security it provided, I'd be out of there so fast it'd make your head spin."

   *Reflection:*_____

   _____

   Rating:_____

   *Reflection:*_____

   _____

   Rating:_____

   *Reflection:*_____

   _____

   Rating:_____

2. My little girl is so cute. I love to dress her up. I find all these pretty things for her, and friends give me stuff, too. And I can tell she thinks she's cute, too. She really hams it up. But sometimes I wonder if I'm overdoing it.

   *Reflection:*_____

   _____

   Rating:_____

   *Reflection:*_____

   _____

   Rating:_____

   *Reflection:*_____

   _____

   Rating:_____

3. This school sucks. I hate my classes, all of my friends have dropped out already, and I just want to get out of here. I don't know what else I'll do, but I've got to get out of here.

*Reflection:*_____

_____

Rating:_____

*Reflection:*_____

_____

Rating:_____

*Reflection:*_____

_____

Rating:_____

4. Things have gotten tougher at home. I think he's drinking more, although I can never be sure because he doesn't drink much when he's around me. But he's getting home later and later, and when he does get home, I know he's been drinking.

*Reflection:*_____

_____

Rating:_____

*Reflection:*_____

_____

Rating:_____

*Reflection:*_____

_____

Rating:_____

5. She is such a whiner. No matter what I do it's not right. Last night, for example, I made this great Italian dish, and she complained that it was too salty. It's always something.

*Reflection:*_____

_____

Rating:_____

*Reflection:*_____

_____

Rating:_____

*Reflection:*_____

_____

Rating:_____

More Reflections—This Time With Feeling

Thus far your reflection work has focused on capturing the meaning of what a client says and then accurately formulating a way of reflecting that. You can also use reflections to respond to your client's feelings. By using feelings words—sad, mad, glad, scared, and all of their variants—you can, even more than when accurately reflecting meaning, demonstrate your capacity for understanding your client's internal world.

Good reflections can help your client begin to understand her feelings, both by naming them and by seeing how they are attached to the events of her life. Your reflections can help her to sort out the complex mix of feelings that sometimes accompany thoughts about people and how they interact with her. For people who seem adrift in a sea of feelings, these reflections can help to create some order and a beginning sense of control; for people who have difficulty expressing feeling, your reflections can begin to help give voice to what has been unexpressed.

Perhaps the best way to explore these varieties of feelings reflections is by way of example. . . .

Reflections of Feelings Examples

You have a 7th-grade boy in your office. He's been referred to you because he was caught fighting in the cafeteria. As he starts to talk with you, he tears up, and says, "I wasn't doing anything. I try to avoid these guys, but they always seem to know where I am. They try to take my money, and they're always just bumping me around. Today I tried to stick up for myself and I got blamed. It's just not fair!"

You might respond with these *reflections of feeling*:

1. It's scary having a bunch of guys on your case.

2. This seems really unfair, and it's really frustrating.

3. Being scared and mad, all scrambled in together.

What do you think of these responses? Can you see yourself using any of these? Notice that you would be supplying words for feelings that he has not articulated. You're using your best guesses to try to accurately surmise what's going on inside. You can use your own thoughts about what it would be like to be in his position as your guide for what kinds of feelings words you might want to use.

List two other alternative *reflections of feeling* that you might use in this situation:

1. _____

_____

2. _____

_____

Here's another situation:

A new client has been talking about her difficult and complicated relationship with her mother. She has described how her mother demands attention and assistance but then rejects help when it's offered. The mother's health is failing and she can no longer care for herself. Your client is caught between trying to care for her own family and dealing with her mother. She says, "It's unbelievable! I'm trying to raise my kids, have some kind of a relationship with my husband, and here she is calling every five minutes . . . asking for this, asking for that, telling me I need to do more to help her. And then when I do it, whatever she's asking for, it's never quite right. What the heck am I supposed to do?!"

Here are some possible *reflections of feeling* for this situation:

1. This is really tough, really hard.

2. It's enough to make you sad, mad . . . all kinds of things.

3. It's incredibly frustrating.

What do you think of these? Note, again, that you are supplying words for feelings that she has not used. Your best attempts to do this will relate to your ability to identify with her situation and to imagine the feelings she might be feeling. If you can accurately identify and give voice to those feelings, it will generally be received as a great gift . . . the gift of being truly understood.

List two other alternative *reflections of feeling* that you might use in this situation:

1. _____

_____

2. _____

_____

Reflections of Content and Feeling

The best way of responding to someone, almost regardless of what he is telling you about, is to accurately reflect both the content of what is being said and the feelings associated with what's being discussed. These *reflections of content and feeling* really serve to connect you to your client. This is the grandmother of all counseling skills, at least those related to relationship development. If you only have one tool in your counseling skill toolbox, have this one. The degree to which you do this well—reflect content and feeling—will have a great deal to do with how successful your counseling relationship will be. Moreover, this skill, when applied to friendships and love relationships, will help all of those relationships improve.

Reflections of Content and Feeling Examples

Let's consider the same two case examples just reviewed. The first, having to do with the middle school-aged boy who'd been caught fighting. He says, "I wasn't doing anything. I try to avoid these guys, but they always seem to know where I am. They try to take my money, and they're always just bumping me around. Today I tried to stick up for myself and I got blamed. It's just not fair!"

Here are some possible *reflections of content and feeling*:

1. You finally decide to stand up to these bullies, and then you're the one who gets punished. Frustrating!

2. It's really scary dealing with these guys . . . they really seem to have it in for you.

3. It's like nobody's on your side. Not these kids who are after you, and not the teachers who blamed you for fighting. Pretty lonely.

In your attempt to capture both the meaning and feeling of what's been said, and then reflecting it, your responses may be a little longer. Try your best to keep your responses as short as possible, remembering that the more you say the more the risk is that the focus will be shifted away from your client towards you.

Suggest a couple of other reflections of content and feeling that you might use for this situation:

Alternative 1.

_____

_____

_____

Alternative 2.

_____

_____

_____

And then there is the case of the daughter and her demanding mother. The daughter, your client, is discussing her difficult situation. She says, "It's unbelievable! I'm trying to raise my kids, have some kind of a relationship with my husband, and here she is calling every five minutes . . . asking for this, asking for that, telling me I need to do more to help her. And then when I do it, whatever she's asking for, it's never quite right. What the heck am I supposed to do?!"

Here are some possible *reflections of content and feeling* you might use:

1. You're stuck between the needs of your family and your demanding mom . . . man, this is maddening.

2. No matter how much you do for her, it's never enough. Exhausting.

3. You give the word "supermom" new meaning. What a lot to manage! Exhausting and infuriating!

What do you think of these? Would you use any of them?

You can deliver these reflections with a fair amount of confidence of their accuracy. So they don't need to be posed as questions, or with voice inflections that sound tentative. Your client will eventually correct you if you are inaccurate.

Now suggest a couple of other reflections of content and feeling that you might use for this situation:

Alternative 1.

_____

_____

_____

Alternative 2.

_____

_____

_____

EXERCISE: CREATING AND RATING YOUR REFLECTIONS OF CONTENT AND FEELING

Following are a number of examples of things your new clients might be saying to you. With each of these pose three alternative *reflections*. Rate each of your *reflections of content and feeling,* as follows: +1 (accurate and additive); 0 (neutral, does not distort, does not add); or −1 (distorts and detracts):

1. My colleague is a weasel. I do the work, she takes the credit, and then she bad-mouths me behind my back.

   *Reflection of content and feeling:*_____

   _____

   Rating:_____

   *Reflection of content and feeling:*_____

   _____

   Rating:_____

   *Reflection of content and feeling:*_____

   _____

   Rating:_____

2. My 16-year-old is learning how to drive. I want her to get her license so she can truck herself around to where she needs to go, but I worry about what she'll do when she's out of sight.

   *Reflection of content and feeling:*_____

   _____

   Rating:_____

   *Reflection of content and feeling:*_____

   _____

   Rating:_____

   *Reflection of content and feeling:*_____

   _____

   Rating:_____

3. I've been here for a little over a year. My language isn't so good and I'm having a hard time finding a job. It's all so different.

*Reflection of content and feeling:*_____

_____

Rating:_____

*Reflection of content and feeling:*_____

_____

Rating:_____

*Reflection of content and feeling:*_____

_____

Rating:_____

4. Law school is unbelievably hard, and competitive. I never feel like I've done enough; there's always more. And my family has done so much to help me get here; I don't know what I'd do if I fail.

*Reflection of content and feeling:*_____

_____

Rating:_____

*Reflection of content and feeling:*_____

_____

Rating:_____

*Reflection of content and feeling:*_____

_____

Rating:_____

5. I bet you've never tried living on welfare. Month to month, what's it going to be . . . food, or rent, or check-ups for the baby? I can't believe people think people on welfare are getting a good deal.

*Reflection of content and feeling:*_____

_____

Rating:_____

*Reflection of content and feeling:*_____

_____

Rating:_____

*Reflection of content and feeling:*_____

_____

Rating:_____

**DVD
Observation
of Reflection
of Content
and Feeling**

Watch the role play entitled, "Assessment and Counseling With a Grieving Client" on the DVD that accompanies the text, *The Essential Counselor.* In this counseling session, David is role playing a man whose wife has recently died. Jane, his counselor, is trying to establish a relationship with him, and she is also trying to assess the nature and severity of his grief. After you've finished watching this session—and feel free to watch the review/feedback session, as well—respond to the following:

1. Cite two or three *reflections of content, or of content and feeling,* that Jane uses in this session.

_____

_____

_____

2. How effective do you think these were?

_____

_____

_____

3. Create one *reflection of content and feeling* that you might say to David as this session ends.

_____

_____

_____

**Role Play Exercise:
Reflections of
Content and Feeling**

For this role play, you'll need a partner. It might be someone from your class, or it might be a friend or relative.

Have your partner think of some situation at home or at work that he or she can talk about for approximately 5 minutes. This should not be a situation that holds too much emotion or difficulty for your partner. It might involve, for example, describing an upcoming work project, or simply talking about other people with whom work is shared.

Your job is to respond to your partner's description of this situation using *reflections*—only *reflections.* Really—try to ask no questions, only reflect on what has been said.

Take a few minutes following this conversation to discuss the interaction, focusing primarily on your facility in making *reflections* that felt helpful to your partner.

How accurate were they? Did they serve to move the conversation along, hopefully in an ever more meaningful direction? Were there difficulties? What might become problematic if only reflections are used during the course of a counseling session?

Then swap roles with your partner and do it again.

When the role plays and discussion of them are completed, note some final comments and reflections in the space provided below. Then fill out the personal assessment question and comment section that follows. Finally, swap your assessments with a student colleague or give it to your instructor. This other person can add her thoughts to your assessment, and you may be reviewing hers.

Role Play Comments:

_____

_____

_____

_____

Concluding Personal Assessment: Reflections of Content and Feeling

Name _____

Which of the following statements best reflects how well you think you understand and will be able to accurately utilize these skills? Circle one:

1. I believe that I quite thoroughly understand these skills, and I know that I will be able to use them in my work with clients.

2. I understand these skills, but am not sure about how well I'll be able to use them in my counseling work.

3. I'm still pretty unclear about what these skills are all about, and I'm not sure about how to use them.

Comments:

_____

_____

_____

_____

Concluding Peer and/or Instructor Assessment: Reflections of Content and Feeling

Which of the following statements best reflects how well you think this person understands and will be able to accurately utilize these skills? Circle one:

1. I believe that this person clearly understands these skills, and I am confident that he/she will be able to use them in his/her work with clients.

2. These skills are understood, but am not sure about how well he/she will be able to use them in his/her counseling work.

3. He/she is still pretty unclear about these skills and their use.

Comments:

_____

_____

_____

_____

Reviewer Name _____

6

Using Little Tools With Big Effect

Silence and Simple Prompts

Introduction

Sometimes less is more, and that is oftentimes the case in developing counseling relationships. It should be obvious that when you are talking less your client is presumably talking more. Most of the work during counseling sessions should be done by your client as she explores aspects of herself and her world. You are there more as a catalyst, someone who can help her to mobilize her own resources to deal with her life situations . . . and less as an expert problem solver.

Naturally, as a fellow traveler on the road of life, you will be able to provide another way of looking at things, and your best role will be that of non-judgmental, accepting listener. The whole job becomes less burdensome when you accept the fact that your primary task is to "be with" her, not "fix" her. As you enter her world and hear her describe what works and doesn't in how she approaches people and the tasks of living, you will be able to provide your own view of that, but it is always important to recall that this really is her world.

The two skills discussed in this chapter are designed to provide your client ample room to explore and discuss whatever has brought her in to counseling. *Silence* is simply not responding, affording her the opportunity to continue, without interference, and *simple prompts* are little encouragements for her to go on talking. Deciding how and when to use each of these skills will become easier as you gain experience.

Silence

There are different kinds of silence. Some silences are filled with anxiety, suggesting tension in the relationship, or simply a not knowing of what to do next. If your client is unsure of what is expected—and this is typically the case with a new client—silences may be uncomfortable and anxiety-ridden. These are typically a cue for you to be more active, to ask questions, or to do some reflecting on what's been discussed. Generally, using *silence as a skill* is something that will be used less at the beginning of a relationship, more as the relationship evolves and your client understands more of what is expected.

Oftentimes new counselors will jump in quickly after a client has begun to discuss something as a way to avoid their own anxiety about quiet moments. You can experiment with pushing yourself to wait a bit after your client or practice partner has said something. See if, by waiting, your client will continue without prompting. You can experiment with pushing your-self to wait a bit after your client or practice partner has said something. See if, by waiting, your client will continue without prompting. You don't want to wait too long, for more anxiety will creep in between you. You also probably won't want to use too much silence with very young children or with people who are severely disturbed; silence will most likely be counter-productive in these situations.

When you do choose to use silence, and your client runs out of gas, doesn't seem to know where to go next and things get uncomfortable, you can always make a *reflection about the silence*, with something like, "It can be hard to figure out where to go next. . . ." This suggests you're actively present, but allows your client to choose the direction of where this goes next.

DVD
Observation of
the Use of Silence

The first role play portrayed on the DVD that accompanies *The Essential Counselor* has to do with engaging a reluctant client. It is entitled, "Engaging a Mandated, Reluctant Client." This role play shows a counselor trying to engage a client who has been referred for counseling by his probation officer. The client is not happy to be in counseling, and the counselor struggles through the first part of the interview to find something that will spark a connection with this reluctant guy. At the 9:35 minute mark of the session, things begin to take a turn. There are two or three pregnant pauses, moments of silence, where the counselor tries to time how much silence is productive, and how much to intervene.

Watch the 5- to 10-minute period of this interview, starting at 9:40, where the counselor tries to use some brief periods of silence. You may want to watch the entire interview leading up to that 5- to 10-minute period to see the context in which these silence periods occur. Make some brief com-ments/observations to the questions below.

How effective was the use of silence in this interview?

_____

_____

Would you have used silence here? More, less?

_____

_____

What might the counselor have done differently?

_____

_____

Could silence have been productively used earlier in the interview?

_____

_____

EXERCISE: COMFORT WITH SILENCE

This expands on an exercise used in the text. The assumption is that the more comfortable you are with silence in your own life, the more you will be able to productively use it as a skill with your clients. We live in a noise-filled world, and finding silent places and opportunities to be quiet can be difficult. For some of us, silence is simply frightening, so the task of befriending silence can be even more of a challenge. This exercise is a structured opportunity to challenge yourself to be quiet.

During the week ahead, take 10 minutes each day to sit in silence in some quiet place. Try to pick the same time each day, some time when you are not so tired you'll simply fall asleep. Perhaps you have some meditative or prayer routine you'd like to use, or perhaps you simply want to sit. This will be your choice. No radio, no television, no computers, phones, or books. No distractions, in other words. At the end of each quiet session, make a few written notes about the experience. At the end of the week, summarize your notes in the space below.

Reflections on spending time in silence:

_____

_____

_____

_____

_____

_____

_____

_____

_____

_____

_____

_____

_____

_____

_____

_____

_____

EXERCISE: THE SKILLFUL USE OF SILENCE

For this experience, you will experiment with a few informal social interactions. You can use family gatherings, parties, or conversations with friends as a vehicle for experimenting with the use of silence. In each of these situations, consciously avoid saying anything in response to what others talk about. Certainly you can take opportunities to talk about yourself as the social interaction unfolds, but try saying nothing in response to others' conversation. You can use nonverbal (head nods, hand gestures, etc.) to show your interest, but do this without words. Try to be as natural with this as possible. If at some point people become curious as to what you're doing, then you can tell them about your experimenting with silence.

After each social interaction where you've experimented with using silence as a responding skill, make some informal notes. At the end of the week, summarize your findings in the space below.

Reflections on using silence in social interactions:

_____

_____

_____

_____

_____

_____

_____

_____

_____

_____

_____

_____

_____

_____

_____

_____

_____

Simple Prompts

A simple prompt is an invitation to continue talking. It is akin to using silence, in that you will not be furnishing more information in way of questions or reflections to which your client can respond. Rather, the simple prompt asks someone to go on, to talk more.

The subtlest simple prompts are little nonverbal actions—a shake of the head, a widening of the eyes, an invitational hand gesture—which suggests that you're ready to hear more. More obvious and direct prompts are verbal, like "Tell me more about that," or "Yes, go on." The function of these prompts is to keep things moving, keep your client exploring and talking, with minimal invasiveness on your part. Because they are not posed as questions, they also serve to help your client stay on topic. If she chooses to shift away from the topic of discussion, that will then be her choice. These nonverbal and verbal prompts also demonstrate that you are actively engaged.

Examples: Simple Prompts

Your client says, "He's so rude! Every time I start to say something he interrupts. I can't believe I'm involved with this guy." Then she stops. Instead of asking a question, you might say one of the following:

1. "Yeah," and give an invitational hand gesture, suggesting she continue.

2. "Go on."

3. "Tell me more about him."

And in another situation, your client says, "I like math ok, but I don't know if that's what I want to study in college. I like other stuff, too. Really liking chemistry this semester, and science, generally. Just not sure." Again, instead of asking questions, you might say one of the following:

1. "Explore this some more."

2. "Keep going."

3. "Interesting," and use head nods and hand gestures to invite her to say more about this.

DVD Observation of the Use of Simple Prompts

The second role play on the DVD that accompanies *The Essential Counselor* is entitled, "Cultural Issues in Counseling With an Adolescent Client." In this interview, where the counselor is trying to both engage her new student client, as well as find out what's been happening in her client's world.

Watch the first 5 to 7 minutes of this interview. It portrays the counselor making a number of simple prompts (which are technically posed as questions) to draw the young woman out and to help her express the dynamics of her school situation. After you have watched this clip, reflect and respond to the following:

1. How effective were these prompts in engaging this student?

_____

_____

_____

2. Could these questions that the counselor uses to prompt be posed as statements? If so, how?

_____

_____

_____

3. What might you have done differently?

_____

_____

_____

EXERCISE: THE USE OF SIMPLE PROMPTS

List three alternative simple prompts, each meant to nudge the client into more discussion and disclosure, to each of the following client interviews.

Your client is the mother of a 12-year-old girl. She says, *"My daughter is starting to really give me a hard time. There's something about girls and their mothers—particularly middle school aged girls and their mothers—I guess, that is usually pretty tough."*

1.

Now circle one of the following numbers:

This prompt will:

1. Help the client go on, moving more deeply into the material.   2. This prompt might shift the focus away from what's been talked about.   3. There's no point in making this comment.

2.

This prompt will:

1. Help the client go on, moving more deeply into the material.   2. This prompt might shift the focus away from what's been talked about.   3. There's no point in making this comment.

3.

This prompt will:

1. Help the client go on, moving more deeply into the material.   2. This prompt might shift the focus away from what's been talked about.   3. There's no point in making this comment.

In the second situation, you have as a client a young man who has been sent to you by his wife. She has been telling him that he doesn't listen to her, and that he needs to improve his listening skills. She's told him that he needs to learn how to communicate better and that the best way to do this will be by talking with a counselor. He says, *"You know, I love her a lot, but sometimes I just don't know what she wants. It seems like nothing I do is enough. I mow the lawn, I work like a dog at my job, and I don't hang around bars. And now she says I don't listen! Women!"*

1.

This prompt will:

1. Help the client go on, moving more deeply into the material.   2. This prompt might shift the focus away from what's been talked about.   3. There's no point in making this comment.

2.

This prompt will:

1. Help the client go on, moving more deeply into the material.   2. This prompt might shift the focus away from what's been talked about.   3. There's no point in making this comment.

3.

This prompt will:

1. Help the client go on, moving more deeply into the material.   2. This prompt might shift the focus away from what's been talked about.   3. There's no point in making this comment.

Role Play Exercise: The Use of Silence and Simple Prompts

For this role play you'll need a partner—someone from class, a friend, or a relative. For 5 minutes your partner should tell you about his or her pets—the ones grown up with, or the current ones. This discussion could include the role and meaning these pets had in the family. Alternatively, if one of you have had no pets, you could talk about a best friend.

As you listen to your partner or a best friend describe these pets, you may respond only with simple prompts and silence. Try to stay with this, even if it gets hard. Try to use the entire 5 minutes, even if things begin to stall. Should that happen, think about how you could use a simple prompt to address the "stalling."

When the role plays and discussion of them are completed, note some final comments and reflections in the space provided below. Then fill out the personal assessment question and comment section that follows. Finally, swap your assessments with a student colleague or give it to your instructor. This other person can add his thoughts to your assessment, and you may be reviewing his.

Role Play Comments:

_____

_____

_____

_____

Concluding Personal Assessment: The Use of Silence and Simple Prompts

Name _____

Which of the following statements best reflects how well you think you understand and will be able to accurately utilize these skills? Circle one:

1. I believe that I quite thoroughly understand these skills, and I know that I will be able to use them in my work with clients.

2. I understand these skills, but am not sure about how well I'll be able to use them in my counseling work.

3. I'm still pretty unclear about what these skills are all about, and I'm not sure about how to use them.

Comments:

_____

_____

_____

_____

Concluding Peer and/or Instructor Assessment: The Use of Silence and Simple Prompts

Which of the following statements best reflects how well you think this person understands and will be able to accurately utilize these skills? Circle one:

1. I believe that this person clearly understands these skills, and I am confident that he/she will be able to use them in his/her work with clients.

2. These skills are understood, but am not sure about how well he/she will be able to use them in his/her counseling work.

3. He/she is still pretty unclear about these skills and their use.

Comments:

_____

_____

_____

_____

Reviewer Name _____

7

Hunches, Challenges, and the Use of Paradox

Introduction

These skills begin to utilize, in a somewhat larger fashion, some of your own thinking about your client and the situations he confronts. They are designed to stimulate client thought, particularly to look at the world in ways that are different than the customary patterns into which your client's thoughts may have fallen.

A *hunch* invites your client to speculate with you about the meaning of something, or about the way a particular problem has been viewed. A *challenge*, a gentle verbal nudge, urges your client to rethink some closely held idea, value, or behavior; and a *paradox* turns a set of ideas on their head. Let's consider each of these, in turn.

The Hunch

The *hunch* is a tool that you can use to interject some of your own thinking into an interaction with a client in a way that doesn't sound presumptuous or come off as sounding too heavy handed. It is a means for you to provide another way for your client to look at something, a strategy for turning you into a co-conspirator with your client as you try to examine the meaning of what this is all about. You could, of course, begin to approach the same information by using questions, but this is more direct, and will also make you sound more confident.

While there are wide varieties of language that can be used to pose some kind of *hunch*, one of the easiest ways to do this is to start a statement with the phrase, "I wonder what would happen . . . ," and then following with the specifics of the idea you have.

Examples: Using Hunches

Each of the following client statements is followed with a variety of counselor *hunches*. See which, if any, of these, are statements you would feel comfortable making.

Your client says, "My boss is always after me about something. I try my best, but I never quite get it right. If I try to work too fast I make mistakes.

If I slow down to get it right, I miss deadlines. It's a no-win situation. I sometimes think the best thing to do would be to quit."

In response, you might say:

1. "I wonder what his issue is, what he's got going on."
2. "I wonder what would happen if you were to confront him, or have a serious conversation about all of this."
3. "I wonder why the only option seems to be quitting."

How do these sound to you? What alternatives might you use? List two:

1. _____

   _____

   _____

   _____

2. _____

   _____

   _____

   _____

Another way to pose a *hunch* is to start your statement with "It's interesting that . . . ," or "It's curious that . . . ," or some other variant on the theme. So in response to the same client issues with the boss, you might say:

1. "It's curious that there are these difficulties, but you don't talk with him about the problems."
2. "It's interesting that you'd consider quitting before talking with him about this."

How do these *hunches* sound? Could you see yourself using these?

And, finally, you could link these *hunches* together: "It's interesting that you'd consider quitting before you'd talk with him about all this. I wonder what that's about." In this way you begin to become a partner in exploring the meaning of the relationship she has with her boss, as well as providing a springboard toward looking at her attitudes and issues regarding her work situation.

Here's another one for you. Your client says, "I just can't figure out what I want to do. I'm pretty good with my hands, I like to fix things, but I don't have any training in any special area. I'm thinking I'd make a good car mechanic, or even something like welding or plumbing, but I just don't know. My parents just want me to go to college."

List three alternative *hunches* you might make . . . and then rate them by circling the appropriate number:

1. _____

_____

_____

This hunch: 1. Will prod her in a helpful direction.   2. Is interesting, but probably won't have much impact.   3. Is negative, and might push her away.

2. _____

_____

_____

This hunch: 1. Will prod her in a helpful direction.   2. Is interesting, but probably won't have much impact.   3. Is negative, and might push her away.

3. _____

_____

_____

This hunch: 1. Will prod her in a helpful direction.   2. Is interesting, but probably won't have much impact.   3. Is negative, and might push her away.

Using Challenges

Challenging your client, similar to using hunches, is letting your client know that you have some thoughts about her and her situation. In addition to speculating with her about these issues, however, you are giving her a gentle push in one direction or another. Oftentimes this may be to encourage your client to look at some behavior that is not working well, or conversely, it may be to help her acknowledge some hidden strengths.

The use of *challenges* should be undertaken carefully, even gently. You are perceived by your client as a powerful person, and you want to use that perceived power wisely. Your *challenges* will engage that part of her that knows exactly what you're talking about: her problematic work behavior, her drinking or drug problems, her strengths as a colleague and professional, for example.

Your *challenges* may sometimes be directive (strongly suggesting some course of action, like "You really need to stop using drugs!"), but should not be confrontational. You are looking to align yourself with your client—remember the therapeutic alliance—not beat her up. Confrontation suggests judgment, and an "I know better" attitude. While confrontation may yield some quick results in changing behavior, rarely are those changes long lasting.

Examples:
Using Challenges

You are working as a school counselor in a high school. You have a student who has a lot of trouble standing up for herself . . . with girl friends, with boy friends, with teachers, with parents. She is smart, athletic, and has many skills in a variety of areas. You have a good, longstanding relationship with her. She knows that you like her. One day she comes into your office, sits down, and says, "Sam (her boyfriend) did it again. He asked me to meet him at 7 at the movies last Friday night, and then he never showed up. He just treats me like dirt. He thinks he can do anything and I'll take it," and then she starts to cry.

You might, in *challenging* her, say any of the following:

1. "Such a talented, skilled young woman . . . but who lets herself be treated like a door mat."

2. "I sure don't want to tell you what to do, but it seems to me that letting this kind of stuff continue to go on is just plain weird. I wonder what stops you from confronting him?"

3. "You know what you need to do, but for some reason you just don't do it."

   Note that these last two responses are also *hunches,* in that they ask your student client to reflect on the meaning of what she does. *Hunches and challenges* can oftentimes go hand in hand.

What do you think of these responses? Would you be gentler, tougher, or perhaps see these issues in a somewhat different light? Please articulate you reflections about these responses here:

_____

_____

_____

And now list two alternative responses to this young woman you might make, using *challenges,* and then rate them by circling the appropriate number:

1. _____

   _____

   _____

This challenge: 1. Will prod her in a helpful direction. 2. Is interesting, but probably won't have much impact. 3. Is negative, and might push her away.

2. _____

_____

This challenge: 1. Will prod her in a helpful direction.   2. Is interesting, but probably won't have much impact.   3. Is negative, and might push her away.

Now here is another situation, this time with a college student. This student gets good grades, has a number of good friends, and is on two varsity sports teams. He says, "I'm about to graduate and I'm really scared. I haven't even thought about graduate school, and I don't know what I'll do for work. My friends have already got it all worked out. They know exactly what they'll be doing."

List two alternative responses to this student you might make, using *challenges*, and then rate them by circling the appropriate number:

1. _____

_____

_____

This challenge: 1. Will prod him in a helpful direction.   2. Is interesting, but probably won't have much impact.   3. Is negative, and might push him away.

2. _____

_____

_____

This challenge: 1. Will prod him in a helpful direction. 2. Is interesting, but probably won't have much impact.   3. Is negative, and might push him away.

Using Paradox

While the use of *paradox* is discussed a little later in *The Essential Counselor*, its use is included for discussion here because of its close affiliation and potential use in conjunction with *challenges* and *hunches*. *Paradox* is also used in the video clip you are about to watch.

Paradox is the intentional dramatization or exaggeration of some client issue, typically some absurd extension of the issue.

For a client who has trouble with authority, a statement incorporating *paradox* might urge the client to succumb to any suggestion a person in authority might make. *Paradox* might encourage someone who has diffi-culty saying no to requests for help to say "yes" to absolutely every request for assistance, no matter how outrageous. For your client who is hopelessly in love with someone who isn't responding to his overtures of affection, *paradox* might suggest that during the next few weeks your client should think about her during every waking moment.

This is a skill that should be used sparingly and judiciously. In no way should a client be able to interpret your suggestions as actually serious, or as embarrassing. The *paradox* is, in fact, a gentle challenge . . . and should not be heard by your client as a confrontation.

DVD Observation of the Uses of Hunches, Challenges, and Paradox

Get ready to watch the entire DVD role play entitled, "Counseling a High Functioning Adult Client." In this role play, David is counseling Anne, who is role playing a woman at midlife who is grappling with what she wants to do next with her life.

You'll be asked to reflect on a number of questions about the role play when you've finished watching it. You can best prepare for this by first reviewing the following questions regarding this counseling interaction, and then by making notes while you watch the role play.

1. What are this client's primary issues?

   _____

   _____

   _____

2. Identify the hunches and challenges the counselor used to help the client explore these issues. Did you think these were effective? How else might you have used hunches or challenges to help her?

   _____

   _____

   _____

3. There is one use of paradox in this role play. Can you identify it? What did you think about its use here?

   _____

   _____

   _____

4. The counselor has chosen to focus on the issue of the client's sense of emptiness, of not knowing what to do with herself when she's not working or caring for her family. Is this what you would do? If not, in what different direction might you take this?

_____

_____

_____

5. At one point the client asks about medication. How did you think the counselor handled this? Did you agree?

_____

_____

_____

6. The counselor uses some humor in the session. Is this appropriate?

_____

_____

_____

7. Towards the end of the session, the client starts to talk about some things that spark her interest. These things might hold some hope as to how she can mobilize her energies and help her deal with her sense of emptiness. What are these, and what implications do these have for how you would imagine this counseling process would hold in the future? Further, what do you think her sense of "emptiness" is all about? What's your theory about this?

_____

_____

_____

Role Play: Hunches and Challenges

Find a partner with whom you can do a practice role play utilizing _hunches and challenges_. This might be someone from your class or a friend. Ask your partner to consider where he or she might be in 10 years, and what he or she might be doing at that time. Then take 5 to 10 minutes to interview your partner about this vision of the future. Do what you can to interject at least two or three _hunches_ into this interview. If possible, also use a _challenge_ or two. Then take a few minutes to review the session and to allow for feedback. When you have finished with this, swap roles and do another role play.

When the role plays and discussion of them are completed, note some final comments and reflections in the space provided below. Then fill out the personal assessment question and comment section that follows. Finally, swap your assessments with a student colleague or give it to your instructor. This other person can add their thoughts to your assessment, and you may be reviewing theirs.

Comments About the Role Play:

_____

_____

_____

_____

Concluding Personal Assessment: Hunches, Challenges, and the Use of Paradox

Name _____

Which of the following statements best reflects how well you think you understand and will be able to accurately utilize these skills? Circle one:

1. I believe that I quite thoroughly understand these skills, and I know that I will be able to use them in my work with clients.

2. I understand these skills, but am not sure about how well I'll be able to use them in my counseling work.

3. I'm still pretty unclear about what these skills are all about, and I'm not sure about how to use them.

Comments:

_____

_____

_____

_____

Concluding Peer and/or Instructor Assessment: Hunches, Challenges, and the Use of Paradox

Which of the following statements best reflects how well you think this person understands and will be able to accurately utilize these skills? Circle one:

1. I believe that this person clearly understands these skills, and I am confident that he/she will be able to use them in his/her work with clients.

2. These skills are understood, but am not sure about how well he/she will be able to use them in his/her counseling work.

3. He/she is still pretty unclear about these skills and their use.

Comments:

_____

_____

_____

_____

Reviewer Name _____

8

Making It Personal

Affirming and Promoting Immediacy

Introduction

You've asked your new client intelligent questions. You've reflected what she has told you in a way that demonstrates your interest and understanding, and you have also begun to gently challenge some of her assumptions about herself in the world. You have begun to create an environment where your client can experience you as a trustworthy person. With this capacity to trust comes an ability to become more vulnerable and to show parts of her inner self that are not usually viewed by others.

You want to fully support this client's exploration and increasing vulnerability. You can do this by becoming even more of an ally in your support for the work she's doing. Three closely related skills for assisting this support are discussed in *The Essential Counselor – affirming, validating, and cheerleading*. The distinctions between these are subtle. *Affirming* means providing support by telling your client that you believe she has the skills and the wherewithal to do something she wants to do. It's encouragement. *Cheerleading* is encouragement too, but more forceful – "I know you can do it! Go for it!"

And *validation* is providing support by way of understanding and confirming your client's description of her experiences or her internal emotional state. Many of our clients have come from backgrounds where their emotional world has not been validated, where they learn to not trust either other people or even their own ideas about their own internal worlds. Your *validation* of how she views her world can be a great counterbalance to all of the negativity she's experienced.

Using any of these—*affirmation, validation*, or *cheerleading*—puts you solidly in your client's camp. It establishes your belief in her capacity to see her world accurately and to act positively on her own behalf. Your client may not have had many people in her life who have believed in her, and your support could be a wonderful asset.

Another way of making this counseling process with her more personal, where again you are becoming ever more closely allied with her, is by *promoting immediacy* in the relationship. If you operate under the assumption that much of how your client talks about her life in the world is actually replicated in a tangible, real way between the two of you, you can occasionally point that out to her. If she talks about difficulties in relationships with people, for example, some of those same difficulties may sometimes rear their head in your office. When you point out how that is happening, you are *promoting immediacy*. You are bringing the outside inside. This, too, serves to make the relationship more personal, more immediate, more real.

It also can be a great source of immediate learning for her. She now has a direct experience of how her behaviors may impact others.

Let's consider some examples of *affirming* and *promoting immediacy* that may help to make the use of these skills more apparent.

Examples: Using the Skill of Affirming

Following are a number of client comments, followed by two alternative *affirming* responses that a counselor might make. After you've read those, create one of your own, and then rate it. Assume here that the counselor has had some positive counseling history with each client. When you make your response, you can embellish it with imagined information (as is done in the examples), if you want.

Your client says, "I know I deserve a promotion, but I'm so afraid of asking for it."

Here are two alternative ways you might respond to this:

1. You've clearly done the work to deserve this. I know you can do it.

2. You've got the skills, you've got the talent. If they don't see that they're nuts.

Could you see yourself using either of these? Now create one of your own:

Your response:

_____

_____

_____

This affirmation: 1. Will prod her in a helpful direction.   2. Is interesting, but probably won't have much impact.   3. Is negative, and might push her away.

Your next client says, "I know I'm going to flunk that test, I just know it." Here are two alternative ways you might respond:

1. Actually, I think you're going to do fine. You've used the skills you learned in the tutoring center, and you've studied hard. I think you're going to pass it with room to spare.

2. Don't sweat it . . . you'll pass with flying colors.

Could you see yourself using either of these? Now create one of your own:

Your response:

_____

_____

_____

This affirmation: 1. Will prod her in a helpful direction.   2. Is interesting, but probably won't have much impact.   3. Is negative, and might push her away.

And, finally, this client says: "I just don't know how my Dad will take it. I've disappointed him so many times, I just don't know how he'll react." Here are two ways you might respond in an affirming way:

1. Sure, you can't predict how he'll respond, but at least you'll feel good about how much courage you mustered to say it.

2. This is really not as bad as you make it out to be. He might not understand, but at least you'll have it off your chest.

How do these sound to you? Now create your own:

Your response:

_____

_____

_____

This affirmation: 1. Will prod her in a helpful direction.   2. Is interesting, but probably won't have much impact.   3. Is negative, and might push her away.

Affirming: Some Provisos and a Final Thought

You may have noticed in these situations that the affirmations that were made are helping the client prepare for some difficult test or experience. You want to make sure, while you are showing support for your client, that you are not heavily invested in how she does on the task she is about to undertake. You might be happy for her when (if) she passes a test, for example. But you are happy for her because she's happy, not because she passed the test. Your support for her is not conditional upon her performance, in other words. She may, after all, flunk the test. You don't want her to think that you're disappointed in her.

Related to this is the suggestion that you follow your client's lead in her readiness to try something. Be careful about pushing your client into doing something she might not be ready to undertake. Unless she is incapable of making her own decisions, she should be the one deciding when the time is right to try something.

Finally, sometimes it's appropriate—and a terrific addition—if you can include in an affirmation a statement about your own personal liking for your client. This client might not have many friends, and it could be a real boost to hear that you value her. "I think you can do this. I think you're terrific. I like you a lot." Naturally, the statement has to be honestly felt, and can't be overly affectionate or presented in a way that it might be taken inappropriately (e.g., romantically). It also needs to fit in the context of what is happening in the conversation between the two of you.

Examples: Using the Skill of Promoting Immediacy

Following are a number of client comments, followed by two alternative *promoting immediacy* responses that a counselor might make. After you've read those, create one of your own, and then rate it.

Your client has been having difficulty in most of his relationships: his wife, his boss, his children. You've experienced him as a negative person, rarely saying anything positive. He says, "My kids are really screwing up, and they never listen to me."

Here are two different ways you might respond, *promoting immediacy*:

1. That must be really tough, them not listening. I wonder, though, if they hear about the good stuff they do; I notice that with me, at least, you don't say many positive things.

2. You talk a lot about people not listening. I wonder if that happens here, as well—I mean about my not listening well to you.

These are two very different ways of *promoting immediacy*. One is a *gentle challenge*, the other a *hunch*. Do you like either of these? Create one of your own:

Your response:

_____

_____

_____

This statement *promoting immediacy*: 1. Will prod him in a helpful direction. 2. Is interesting, but probably won't have much impact. 3. Is negative, and might push him away.

Another client is a man who says that he has difficulty with women. They seem to avoid him. He's very large, with a booming voice. (You are a woman counselor.) You might respond with a statement *promoting immediacy* by saying:

1. You know, when I first met you, I was intimidated—you're a big guy— but I've come to see you as much more than that. I wonder if other women are intimidated.

2. Maybe women don't have a best first impression. I, for example, was a little put off at first . . . you're such a large presence.

Do you like either of these? Create one of your own:

Your response:

_____

_____

_____

This statement *promoting immediacy*: 1. Will prod him in a helpful direction. 2. Is interesting, but probably won't have much impact. 3. Is negative, and might push him away.

And, finally, in this school counseling example, your student says to you, "My teachers, my parents, they're all the same. They think I'm just a kid, and they never take me seriously." Your alternative *promoting immediacy* statements might be:

1. I wonder if you think that happens here, with me, as well.

2. Maybe you don't think I take you seriously, either.

What do you think of these? Create one of your own:

Your response:

_____

_____

_____

This statement *promoting immediacy*: 1. Will prod him in a helpful direction. 2. Is interesting, but probably won't have much impact. 3. Is negative, and might push him away.

Promoting Immediacy: Concluding Thoughts

This is a skill that should be used judiciously. While you may want to use immediacy, your own reactions to your client, to point out how other people might be reacting to the things he or she does, you don't want this ever to be embarrassing. So, like the skill of giving feedback, you want to avoid judgment. You also want to keep the focus on the client, not have the conversation become more about your reactions. This can be tricky. Do what you can when sharing (self-disclosing) any of your own impressions—impressions that will serve to promote immediacy—to not shift things away toward a discussion about you.

DVD Observation of Affirming and Promoting Immediacy

On the DVD of role plays that accompanies *The Essential Counselor* watch the role play entitled, 'Cultural Issues in Working With an Adolescent Client." You've already watched this at least once, but now you'll be honing in on a separate set of skills. In this role play, you will recall that Jane is acting as an adolescent having some difficulties at her new high school. Anne is serving as her counselor, trying to find out the specifics of what is happening and also trying to make a connection with this young woman.

Watch specifically for Anne's uses of *affirming* and *promoting immediacy*, and make note as you see these used in the interview. Then respond to the following:

1. What were some specific times in this interview that Anne utilized affirmation? Did you think that these were effective?

_____

_____

_____

2. How does Anne promote immediacy in this session with Jane? Was it effective?

_____

_____

_____

3. What might you have done differently?

_____

_____

_____

Other comments about the role play:

_____

_____

_____

_____

Role Play Exercise Using Affirmation and Promoting Immediacy

Find a partner with whom you can do a practice role play utilizing the skills of *affirmation* and *promoting immediacy*. This might be someone from your class or a friend. You could utilize the Lab Practice Model for this, too.

Ask your partner to consider talking about some new thing that he or she would like to try to do some time in the future. This could be something physical, something academic, maybe something musical. It would involve a bit of risk, because it has been untried, but something possible, in reach.

Then take 10 to 20 minutes to interview your partner about this vision of trying to do this. Do what you can to interject at least two or three *affirmations* into this interview. Feel free to utilize your overall experience of this person in how you think about posing your *affirmations*.

If possible, also take a shot at *promoting immediacy*. Given the topic of this role play, this may be difficult, but depending on where the interview goes, it may be possible. Try it, if you can.

Then take a few minutes to review the session and to allow for feedback. When you have finished with this, swap roles and allow the other(s) a try at this.

When the role plays and discussion of them are completed, note some final comments and reflections in the space provided below. Then fill out the personal assessment question and comment section that follows. Finally, swap your assessments with a student colleague or give it to your instructor. This other person can add their thoughts to your assessment, and you may be reviewing theirs.

Comments About the Role Play:

_____

_____

_____

_____

Concluding Personal Assessment: Using Affirmations and Promotion of Immediacy

Name _____

Which of the following statements best reflects how well you think you understand and will be able to accurately utilize these skills? Circle one:

1. I believe that I quite thoroughly understand these skills, and I know that I will be able to use them in my work with clients.

2. I understand these skills, but am not sure about how well I'll be able to use them in my counseling work.

3. I'm still pretty unclear about what these skills are all about, and I'm not sure about how to use them.

Comments:

_____

_____

_____

_____

Concluding Peer and/or Instructor Assessment: Using Affirmations and Promotion of Immediacy

Which of the following statements best reflects how well you think this person understands and will be able to accurately utilize these skills? Circle one:

1. I believe that this person clearly understands these skills, and I am confident that he/she will be able to use them in his/her work with clients.

2. These skills are understood, but am not sure about how well he/she will be able to use them in his/her counseling work.

3. He/she is still pretty unclear about these skills and their use.

Comments:

_____

_____

_____

_____

Reviewer Name _____

9

Ethical and Cultural Issues

Introduction to Ethical Issues

You will want to do your work with clients in a way that is not harmful. Good counseling work can only be done in an environment that is safely contained by some standards of good practice. These standards protect the privacy and integrity of the relationship. You will want to familiarize yourself with the *ethical standards* of your helping profession (e.g., the American Counseling Association) and then abide by them when working with people.

Ethical standards serve the purpose of protecting your client, you, and the profession. Codes of ethics help to ensure that the work you do serves to keep your client, you, and the profession safe. Your coursework which is specific to discussion of these ethical principles will help you learn about the range of issues you may encounter, but you don't need to wait for the coursework. You can go online (the American Counseling Association website) and examine the counseling profession's codes now, and then use them to think about the dilemmas that will be posed following this overview.

Resolving Ethical Dilemmas

There are a number of ethical dilemmas posed in the text, *The Essential Counselor*. Here is another set of dilemmas, designed to expand your thinking about the range of ethical concerns that you may encounter. Each of the following ethical dilemmas may pose significant challenges for you, the counselor. Your job here is to think through the specific situation that is presented (acknowledging that you don't have much information to go on), look for appropriate and relevant principles in the codes of ethics and then formulate a response.

Some of the dilemmas here involve *cultural concerns*. You will naturally want your counseling services to be open to all kinds of people, to people who are invariably different in some way from you. There are times when this may introduce some interesting challenges that may become ethical dilemmas.

When you have completed all or some of these dilemmas, you could swap responses with a colleague to check each other's ideas about them. Alternatively, your instructor may want to read your responses.

Ethical Dilemma 1: Your client is requesting access to her file. You have written some things in your case notes that you think might not be helpful to have her read.

You would:

_____

_____

_____

Peer/Instructor Feedback:

_____

_____

_____

Ethical Dilemma 2: Your client brings you a huge bouquet of flowers.

You would:

_____

_____

_____

Peer/Instructor Feedback:

_____

_____

_____

Ethical Dilemma 3: Your client is a very successful investment broker. She suggests that she knows about a good investment possibility. She'd like you to become her partner in pursuing this venture.

You would:

_____

_____

_____

Peer/Instructor Feedback:

_____

_____

_____

Ethical Dilemma 4: You are about to go on vacation. One of your clients calls you in a panic, saying that he has had a crisis in his living situation, and needs to see you. You really don't have time.

You would:

_____

_____

_____

Peer/Instructor Feedback:

_____

_____

_____

Ethical Dilemma 5: You work in a community mental health clinic. One of your wealthy clients is very pleased with how the counseling is going. She offers you an extra check as a token of her appreciation. She says if you don't want to keep it you could donate it to your favorite charity.

You would:

_____

_____

_____

Peer/Instructor Feedback:

_____

_____

_____

Ethical Dilemma 6: You are working in a group private practice. Your client has an organic farm. She wants to barter farm produce, like eggs, meat, and vegetables for counseling services. (You're not a vegetarian.)

You would:

_____

_____

_____

Peer/Instructor Feedback:

_____

_____

_____

Ethical Dilemma 7: You bump into someone who used to be your client at a party. The two of you strike up a conversation, and it quickly appears that there is some "chemistry" between the two of you.

You would:

_____

_____

_____

Peer/Instructor Feedback:

_____

_____

_____

Ethical Dilemma 8: One of your clients is elderly and very sick. He has been receiving radiation and chemotherapy for cancer. He says that he is lonely, tired of being in pain, and has nothing to live for. He wants to end his life.

You would:

_____

_____

_____

Peer/Instructor Feedback:

_____

_____

_____

Ethical Dilemma 9: One of your clients says that she is being discriminated against, and is also being sexually harassed, at her work site.

You would:

_____

_____

_____

Peer/Instructor Feedback:

_____

_____

_____

Ethical Dilemma 10: Your client tells you that he's dealing drugs.

You would:

_____

_____

_____

Peer/Instructor Feedback:

_____

_____

_____

Ethical Dilemma 11: One of your clients tells you that she had "relations" with a former counselor. She says that this was a sexual relationship.

You would:

_____

_____

_____

Peer/Instructor Feedback:

_____

_____

_____

Ethical Dilemma 12: You find out that one of your clients is HIV positive, and he says that he is having unprotected sex.

You would:

_____

_____

_____

Peer/Instructor Feedback:

_____

_____

_____

Ethical Dilemma 13: One of your clients, someone who has been working hard in counseling, says she can no longer afford to come for counseling.

You would:

_____

_____

_____

Peer/Instructor Feedback:

_____

_____

_____

Ethical Dilemma 14: Your client tells you that she's pregnant. You know that she's also still using drugs.

You would:

_____

_____

_____

Peer/Instructor Feedback:

_____

_____

_____

Ethical Dilemma 15: Your client has completed the work she says she wanted to do in counseling. All of her goals for counseling have been met, yet she says she really enjoys you and wants to continue.

You would:

_____

_____

_____

Peer/Instructor Feedback:

_____

_____

_____

Ethical Dilemma 16: You have a new client who has perpetrated some really terrible physical and sexual offenses against children. You are revolted by some of the things he has done.

You would:

_____

_____

_____

Peer/Instructor Feedback:

_____

_____

_____

Ethical Dilemma 17: You work in a small city which has a large Asian American population, yet your agency has very few Asian American clients. You—and none of your colleagues—are Asian American.

You would:

_____

_____

_____

Peer/Instructor Feedback:

_____

_____

_____

Ethical Dilemma 18: You work in a community mental health clinic. You have a new client, a 16-year-old young woman, who is pregnant. She says she wants to have an abortion.

You would:

_____

_____

_____

Peer/Instructor Feedback:

_____

_____

_____

Ethical Dilemma 19: One of your school counseling colleagues tells a sexist joke in front of other staff and students.

You would:

_____

_____

_____

Peer/Instructor Feedback:

_____

_____

_____

Ethical Dilemma 20: You take a new job working at a counseling center that serves a large refugee population, people primarily from Eastern Europe and a variety of countries in Africa. You were brought up and have always lived in this country.

You would:

_____

_____

_____

Peer/Instructor Feedback:

_____

_____

_____

Group Discussion: Ethical and Cultural Issues

Get together in a small group with a few of your student colleagues. Some of the dilemmas posed above, particularly the last five to seven of them, present some interesting cultural issues. Discuss within the group any of these that seem particularly interesting or challenging for you. Take 10 minutes, or so, for this.

Next, brainstorm a list of all cultural differences that exist in your community (e.g., racial, ethnic, physical, religious, etc.). Then discuss what implications this has for doing counseling in this community, particularly for each of you in this group. Take another 15 to 20 minutes for this discussion. Then take a few minutes to write some personal reflections about this group discussion.

Discussion Reflections:

_____

_____

_____

Personal Cultural Education Ideas

What can you do to expand your own cultural horizons in a way that will better enable you to understand the diverse needs of your counseling clientele?

What are some of the things you could do to increase your multicultural understanding, particularly in regards to where and how you see yourself eventually doing counseling work. List some of those ideas here:

_____

_____

_____

Role Play: Cultural Concerns

Find a partner with whom you can do a practice role play utilizing these personal cultural education ideas you've just generated. This will most likely be someone from your class. Each of you should take 15 minutes to describe, in turn, your ideas about what you can do to expand your cultural horizons. This conversation will invariably include your ideas about the kind of work you'll be doing. When you are in the counselor role, use all of the skills at your disposal to help the other person describe his/her ideas. Experiment with the different skills that you've learned. Then take a few minutes to review each session and to allow for feedback.

When the role plays and discussion of them are completed, note some final comments and reflections in the space provided below. Then fill out the personal assessment question and comment section that follows. Finally, swap your assessments with a student colleague or give it to your instructor. This other person can add her thoughts to your assessment, and you may be reviewing hers.

Comments About the Role Play:

_____

_____

_____

_____

Peer/Instructor Comments:

_____

_____

_____

_____

Concluding Personal Assessment: Ethical and Cultural Concerns

Name _____

Which of the following statements best reflects how well you think you understand and will be able to deal with ethical and cultural issues? Circle one:

1. I believe that I quite thoroughly understand these issues, and I know that I will be able to deal with them in my work with clients.

2. I understand these issues, but am not sure about how well I'll be able to deal with them in my counseling work.

3. I'm still pretty unclear about what these issues are all about, and I'm not sure about how to deal with them.

Comments:

_____

_____

_____

_____

Concluding Peer and/or Instructor Assessment: Ethical and Cultural Issues

Which of the following statements best reflects how well you think this person understands and will be able to accurately deal with ethical and cultural issues? Circle one:

1. I believe that this person clearly understands these issues, and I am confident that he/she will be able to deal with them in his/her work with clients.

2. These skills are understood, but am not sure about how well he/she will be able to deal with them in his/her counseling work.

3. He/she is still pretty unclear about these issues.

Comments:

_____

_____

_____

_____

Reviewer Name _____

10

Dealing With Crisis

Introduction

Regardless of what kind of counseling work you do, you will at some point be called upon to deal with clients in crisis. You may be asked to deal with people who are suicidal, or with someone who is despondent over the loss of a loved one, or with a community reeling from some kind of tragic loss. Crisis can come in all kinds of forms, from those striking individuals to those affecting families, groups, or entire communities.

You may enjoy this kind of counseling work, thriving in the action and drama that is oftentimes involved . . . or you may not enjoy this kind of excitement at all. Whether or not you look forward to the world of crisis counseling, it is best to be as prepared as possible for the inevitable. While having some knowledge and preparation for dealing with crisis may not protect you from the emotional roller coaster crises can provide, that preparation will at least provide you with some tools for responding in a helpful fashion.

The Ingredients of the Successful Crisis Response

Responding to crisis in counseling has been referred to as "providing emotional first aid." This is an apt description of what we do when we respond to crisis. This work is about setting the stage for more long-term assistance, getting someone through a difficult time in order that they can be prepared to undertake the longer term work that needs to be done.

In every crisis situation, there are three important things that need to happen. These are the things you should be prepared to provide. First, the person in crisis needs to feel your *support*. He needs to know that he is not alone, that there is someone present who is helping to shoulder the burden of whatever the crisis is about.

Second, you will need to *explore* the nature of the crisis and this individual's capacity for managing it. This is an assessment process, a survey of internal and external supports and resources, as well as the dynamics of the crisis itself. And, finally, you will want to be able to put together a *plan* for action. What kinds of things will need to happen to get this person through the crisis, and what will happen after the immediate crisis has been brought under control?

Support, exploration, and planning, taken together, make for the effective crisis response. Your ability to be emotionally present in a way that is felt by the person in crisis, your skill in assessing the strengths and resources a person has in managing the crisis—and the potential for harm—as well as your ability to put together a coherent plan for managing this difficult time, will help move someone into a place where more long-term strategies for care can be utilized.

DVD
Observation of
Assessment of a
Client in Crisis

Watch the counseling session entitled, "Assessment and Counseling with a Grieving Client," on the DVD that accompanies the text, *The Essential Counselor.* In this counseling session, Jane is the counselor for David, who is role playing a grieving client, a man whose wife has recently died. After you have finished reviewing the counseling session, respond to the following:

1. What qualifies this as a crisis situation?

   _____

   _____

   _____

2. What are your overall reactions to this session? What did you think about the level of support that was provided? Give examples. What about the plan: Was it specific enough?

   _____

   _____

   _____

3. This role play introduces the threat of suicide as an issue that the counselor must consider. After reviewing what the text, *The Essential Counselor,* has to say about this, how well did you think the counselor responded to this risk in this session?

   _____

   _____

   _____

Now review the feedback/review session for this counseling role play. Are you in agreement with the review of this session, and are there things you would have added, or left out, if you had been there?

_____

_____

_____

Case Discussion: Dealing With Crisis

In this next case example, the counselor is working as part of a disaster relief team. There have been extensive fires in the region, and some people have lost their homes and possessions. As you read the following excerpt of the beginning of one counseling session with a victim of this fire, consider what you might do the same, or differently, and what might come next.

Client: Hi. My name is Mary.

Counselor: Hi Mary. I'm Laurie. Tell me a bit about what's happened and how you are doing.

Client: I can't believe it. My whole world is destroyed. Everything's gone . . . my house, all my things, my cat . . . it's all gone. (She starts to cry.) I wanted to stay to fight the fire, but they wouldn't let me. They told me I had to get out. And now it's all gone.

Counselor: This is really hard. Really hard. It's got to be one of the toughest things anybody would have to go through.

Client: Yeah, it is. I mean, I haven't had an easy life, but this is just too much. It just seems so unfair. So unfair. I even lost my photo albums, pictures of my kids. And now I don't even have a place to stay. I've been staying at the elementary school gym, but now they're saying that we're going to have to move out. (She bangs her fist on the table.) They want to give us money or vouchers so we can find apartments and get food, but I've never been on welfare, or never taken food stamps . . . and I'm not about to start now.

Counselor: This is such a tough situation, maybe harder than anything that's come your way—and you want to somehow get back on your feet, but you're reluctant to take financial help.

Client: I'm no welfare case. I can't stand those losers.

Counselor: You're tough, and you're resilient. And you don't take handouts. But maybe this would be different than taking welfare.

Client: Well, I don't know what you mean, but you're right about me not taking handouts.

Counselor: We can get to that. But also, I would imagine that it's also pretty hard to talk with someone like me, a stranger, in a situation like this, about all this bad stuff that's been happening.

Client: Absolutely. I don't talk to anybody about my problems. I should be able to handle things myself.

Counselor: So, then, I have to tell you how much I admire your courage in being so open with me, particularly when I know that it's not your usual style. I really appreciate your filling me in.

Client: Courage? What's courageous about being up the creek without a paddle? I'm a mess.

Counselor: I think it's really courageous to do something that's hard like this, to talk with someone in a way that's different . . . not asking for help, really, but being open about what's going on. Gutsy.

Client: Hmm.

This brief interchange suggests that the counselor will have her work cut out for her in attempting to encourage this client to accept the help that is being offered. The client is self-reliant, does not like to ask for help, and has been put in a position that is extremely uncomfortable and unfamiliar. The fire was bad enough, but now to be emotionally and financially vulnerable makes the situation almost unbearable.

Did you experience the counselor in this interaction as being supportive? She was attempting to point out that there is courage in vulnerability, in sharing problems with others. This is a notion that runs counter to much of how many people think ("I should be able to solve my problems myself."), and it may be a tough sell with someone who is so fiercely independent.

It will also be a tough sell to encourage this woman to accept financial assistance. Somehow, the current offers of help will have to be "framed" (stated) in a way that don't sound like welfare. Naturally, the counselor may have some very different ideas and values about the whole "welfare" issue, but this is not the time for a discussion about the relative merits of government programs; this is a time to assist this woman in accepting the help that is offered.

What needs to happen next? Assuming the counselor can establish a connection with this client, including offering necessary emotional support, she will then want to find out more about this situation: the specifics of the woman's internal and external support system, what kinds of help have been offered, etc., and then begin to put together, with the client, a plan for action. The action plan will hopefully include accessing the offered help and making arrangement for more counseling contact.

In crisis situations like this, the counselor will most likely have to be more directive than in the other counseling she does. Sometimes people who are not capable of making good decisions when under extreme duress need to be pushed into doing the right thing. A client who is out of control with drug use may need to be coerced into treatment. Someone who is suicidal may need to be forcibly held for a period until the crisis has passed. A client who is homeless because of a fire, even one who is fiercely independent, may need to be strongly encouraged to take financial help.

Comments About This Case Example:

_____

_____

_____

_____

FOR REVIEW: CRISIS SITUATION #1

Consider the following hypothetical situation.

You are a middle school counselor. One of your students has been sent to you by a teacher. The teacher knows that this girl has been bullied—both in person and via social networking—by a group of other girls. The teacher has heard the girl crying, and she's observed her eating alone in the cafeteria. The teacher has heard from other children that the girl has said she wishes she could just disappear. What kinds of things might you say and do for this girl (remember: support, exploration, planning)? Give specific examples in outlining your plan of action, both for when you are with her and for afterwards.

The Plan:

_____

_____

_____

_____

_____

_____

_____

_____

Now trade your plan with one of your colleagues, or hand it in for instructor review. Discuss this, where possible, and make written comments on the other's plan.

Peer/Instructor Review of the Plan:

_____

_____

_____

_____

_____

_____

FOR REVIEW: CRISIS SITUATION #2

Here is another case for your consideration. You work in a drug/alcohol clinic. One of your clients (he's been clean and sober for six months) comes to see you in a state of confusion and disarray. He is unusually disheveled. He says that his wife left him last weekend and that, in response, he got drunk. He says he didn't use any drugs and that he hasn't had anything to drink since that weekend, but he says that he is filled with shame and that he's worried that he'll drink again soon, and maybe go back to using drugs.

   As in the last case situation, put together a plan which includes the emotional and logistical things that should happen. Then swap you plan with a colleague, or have an instructor review it.

The Plan:

_____

_____

_____

_____

_____

_____

_____

_____

_____

Peer/Instructor Review of the Plan:

_____

_____

_____

_____

_____

_____

_____

FOR REVIEW: CRISIS SITUATION #3

In this final crisis case situation, you are a counselor in a community mental health clinic. You've been working for some weeks with a young man who is very depressed. This week he comes in to see you, having just had a routine physical, and the doctor has told him that there are some problems with his blood tests, and that he wants to see him again, soon. Your client is terrified, and he hasn't been eating or sleeping. What would you do?

The Plan:

_____

_____

_____

_____

_____

_____

_____

_____

_____

And, again, trade this with a colleague, or have an instructor review it.

Peer/Instructor Review:

_____

_____

_____

_____

_____

_____

_____

Role Play: Dealing With a Client in Crisis

Find someone who is willing to role play a person in crisis so you can have an opportunity to practice responding. Maybe this will be a friend, maybe a colleague from class. If it's someone from your class, you could take turns being "in crisis."

Here's the situation. This client has just been laid off from the job he (or she) has had for 15 years. There was no hint that this was coming. This person is devastated by the news. There is very little in the way of financial cushion (savings, stocks, etc.), and the job market is bleak. Chances of finding another job quickly are slim. There are young children and a partner at home, and the house is significantly mortgaged.

Your friend/client's job is to assume the feelings of what it would be like to be in this situation. He or she can feel free to embellish the skeleton information about the situation that's presented here with any fictional material that might make this seem more real.

Your job, as the crisis counselor, is to provide support, explore and assess the dynamics of the situation and the resources at this person's disposal, and begin to put together some kind of plan.

This role play can take approximately 15 minutes, with some time spent afterwards for discussion, review, and feedback. Feedback should be particularly focused on helping the counselor recognize those things that were done that seemed to be particularly helpful.

When all of this is completed, please add your comments about your skills as a crisis responder here:

_____

_____

_____

And then swap your comments with a peer, or have this reviewed by an instructor. Peer/instructor comments:

_____

_____

_____

Finally, fill out the personal assessment question and comment section that follows. Then swap your assessments with a student colleague or give it to your instructor. This other person can add their thoughts to your assessment, and you may be reviewing theirs.

_____

_____

_____

Concluding Personal Assessment: Responding to Crisis

Name _____

Which of the following statements best reflects how well you think you understand and will be able to accurately utilize these skills? Circle one:

1. I believe that I quite thoroughly understand these skills, and I know that I will be able to use them in my work with clients.

2. I understand these skills, but am not sure about how well I'll be able to use them in my counseling work.

3. I'm still pretty unclear about what these skills are all about, and I'm not sure about how to use them.

Comments:

_____

_____

_____

_____

Concluding Peer and/or Instructor Assessment: Responding to Crisis

Which of the following statements best reflects how well you think this person understands and will be able to accurately utilize these skills? Circle one:

1. I believe that this person clearly understands these skills, and I am confident that he/she will be able to use them in his/her work with clients.

2. These skills are understood, but am not sure about how well he/she will be able to use them in his/her counseling work.

3. He/she is still pretty unclear about these skills and their use.

Comments:

_____

_____

_____

_____

Reviewer Name _____

11

Working With a Reluctant Client

Introduction

To varying degrees, nearly all of your clients will be reluctant. At least at the beginning, very few people go to see a counselor gleefully. It's usually some kind of difficulty that prompts someone to seek counseling, and knowing that this difficulty will need to get talked about is typically not appealing to most people. It's a little like going to the dentist: We do it in the hopes that we'll feel better afterwards, or in the hopes that we can avoid larger problems.

There are, of course, exceptions. Some school-aged children love to go to see the school counselor. Some adults call a counselor as easily as ordering a pizza. Some people seem to enjoy counseling so much they spend much of their adult lives in counseling with one counselor or another. Some people probably even look forward to going to see the dentist.

But these are the exceptions. Most of our new clients will be reluctant to be seeing us.

As counselors, we hope that as a relationship develops with a new client there will be less reluctance, and that he might even begin to look forward to his visits with us, but we can usually assume that at the outset most of our clients will be approaching us with some trepidation.

Some of your clients will be really, really unhappy about coming for counseling. Some of them will have been coerced, leveraged into counseling by parents, or by the legal system, or by someone who is saying, "You need to get counseling, or else. . . ." Some of these people may be very clear with you about their unhappiness in having to see you, while some others will cover their unhappiness with some kind of protective behavior. Reluctance, or resistance, as we sometimes call it, takes different forms. Let's consider some of these.

Varieties of Reluctance

Some of your clients will be clearly and visibly less than pleased about coming to see you for counseling. They may tell you so directly, or they may simply communicate it in other ways, as with body posture, with facial expressions, or with other nonverbal messages. With this kind of *active reluctance*, or active resistance, at least you know what you've got. This kind of person is letting you know, flat out, that he doesn't want to be here. Oftentimes it is with the coerced client that you will encounter this kind of reluctance.

The other kinds of reluctance can be more insidious, even more difficult with which to deal. These *passive forms of reluctance* are more hidden. With this kind of reluctance a new client might say that he is glad to see you, but act in ways that suggest otherwise. He might flash you a winsome smile, agree with everything you say, and behind that you realize is a resolve to do nothing any differently. Coming late, not participating fully, not paying for services on time—all of these can be interpreted as hidden reluctance. Other kinds of behavior can also be adopted as strategies for covering reluctance—charm, smiling, ready agreement with the best laid plans—all of these can mask an unwillingness to really align with you. And, because it is not so obvious, this kind of reluctance can pose some truly difficult challenges.

Reasons for Reluctance

Why do people act like this? You're a nice person who wants to be helpful. Why don't people just understand that and start dealing with the issues that are giving them difficulty? Why is all of this other defensive, reluctant, behavior happening?

There are usually very good reasons why someone has adopted a "reluctant" stance. Oftentimes people in this person's life have not been trustworthy, or perhaps they've even been mean and abusive. When someone has experienced a lifetime of abuse and trauma—sometimes even at the hands of so-called helping professionals—it is not hard to understand why he is not ready to trust someone new.

You may have some truly bad actors on your caseload, people for whom the word "reluctance" seems far too tame. Typically, behind all of the bravado, manipulative behavior, and other kinds of "reluctance" that these people exhibit are scared and lonely individuals who have experienced a lifetime of abuse.

You will most likely have more people who come to see you who may have done some destructive things (usually to themselves), but who are not so completely defended against the world. They may have had a history of difficult relationships, parents who knew little about parenting, or school and work experiences that were less than satisfying, yet part of them is still yearning for connection and for understanding.

Working With Reluctance

It is always important to remember that reluctance is a learned behavior, and that it was most likely learned as a survival strategy. People who grow up in families where addiction problems run rampant, for example, learn how to behave in ways that have the best chance of minimizing difficulties, like violence. Learning how to be hidden and not trusting are part of such survival strategies, and as a counselor you will have to prove that you are trustworthy before some of those old non-trusting behaviors can be temporarily laid to rest.

There are some things you can do to make contact with and begin to form an alliance with someone who is reluctant:

- Try not to take your client's reluctance personally. Remember this person's history and brush up on your understanding of transference (refer to *The Essential Counselor*). Most of the reluctance has nothing to do with you.
- Make sure that this person is seeing you voluntarily. Even if he or she has been mandated to see a counselor, there should always be a choice, though sometimes the alternatives (like jail) are grim.
- Be as nondefensive as possible. Dealing with reluctance is a bit like a martial art. Using *reflections* can be particularly effective in doing this.
- Look for the hook. Find out something that this person needs from you (e.g., a letter saying she attended counseling that gets sent to a probation officer), and use that as a means to connect.
- You don't need to take over-the-top insulting, rude behavior. You have a right to be treated civilly. You can tell someone who's being truly obnoxious that you won't talk with them until they're ready to treat you with more respect.
- For clients whose reluctance is more hidden, look for warning signs in behaviors that challenge the boundaries of the relationship (e.g., coming late, missing appointments).

Examples: Responding to Reluctance

Following are a few examples of things "reluctant" clients might say to you, with some possible responses you might make. Note that, excepting the response to Client #4, all of the responses are *reflections*. The response to Client #4 combines a *gentle challenge and a hunch*.

Following each of the responses given here, give an alternative one of your own, and then rate its effectiveness by circling the appropriate number.

Client #1:   My PO sent me. (says this while glaring at you.)

Response: This isn't something you'd be choosing to do . . . and it doesn't make you happy.

Your alternative response:

_____

_____

This response: 1. Will prod him in a helpful direction.   2. Is interesting, but probably won't have much impact.   3. Is negative, and might push him away.

Client #2:   My wife thinks I've got a drinking problem. She says I need to get help, so here I am.

Response: It's really tough feeling like you're being forced into coming here.

Your alternative response:

_____

_____

This response: 1. Will prod him in a helpful direction.   2. Is interesting, but probably won't have much impact.   3. Is negative, and might push him away.

Client #3: The principal sent me. I got into a fight, and now she must think I'm psycho to make me come see you.

Response: No fun having to do something you don't want to—especially when you think it's because you think somebody thinks you're nuts.

Your alternative response:

_____

_____

This response: 1. Will prod him in a helpful direction.   2. Is interesting, but probably won't have much impact.   3. Is negative, and might push him away.

Client #4 (You've been seeing this person for a number of weeks.): Great to see you. I've been thinking a lot about what we talked about last week. What a great session. You've really been helpful.

Response: That's terrific. I've noticed, though, that for the last three weeks you've come each time about 10 minutes late and then want to leave early. A lot of times that's a sign that there might be some feelings about coming here that should get talked about. I wonder if that's true for you.

Your alternative response:

_____

_____

This response: 1. Will prod him in a helpful direction.   2. Is interesting, but probably won't have much impact.   3. Is negative, and might push him away.

DVD
Observation of Counseling a Reluctant Client

On the DVD that accompanies *The Essential Counselor* watch the counseling session entitled, "Engaging a Mandated, Reluctant Client." In this counseling role play, Gary is acting as a client who has been sent to a drug and alcohol clinic by his Probation Officer. He is mandated to go for counseling for a fixed number of sessions or he will be sent back to jail. David, as the counselor, is attempting to establish a connection with Gary and is also attempting to do a beginning assessment of what the referral is all about. Take notes, particularly about how David is responding to this reluctant client, and then comment on the following questions.

1. How does this client, verbally and nonverbally, display his "reluctance?"

_____

_____

_____

2. David selectively attends to some material, not all of it (e.g. the "gay" comment). Do you agree with his choices?

_____

_____

_____

3. What is the "hook" that the counselor can use to keep the client engaged? Did the counselor use it appropriately?

_____

_____

_____

4. What did you think about the counselor's use of silence? Was it appropriate?

_____

_____

_____

5. At one point the client started to become more engaged. What happened?

_____

_____

_____

If you haven't already watched the feedback/review session that follows this counseling role play, watch it now. What additional comments might you make?

Comments About the DVD Role Play:

_____

_____

_____

_____

Role Play: Working With a Reluctant Client

Find someone who is willing to role play a reluctant client so you can have an opportunity to practice responding and engaging this kind of person. Maybe this will be a friend, maybe a colleague from class. If it's someone from your class, you could take turns being "in crisis." You might utilize the lab practice model outlined in *The Essential Counselor*.

Here's the situation. Your "client" has been leveraged into counseling by someone else. It might be by a teacher or principal, by an upset spouse or partner, by a work supervisor, or by someone in the legal system. The person who is role playing the client can choose any of these kinds of people, or someone similar, and then should prepare him/herself to "be" that person for a few minutes.

Your friend/client's job is to assume the feelings of what it would be like to be in this situation. He or she can feel free to embellish the skeleton information about the situation with any fictional material that might make this seem more real. He or she should also give you as much information as is necessary to lay the groundwork for this to get started—the kind of counselor you are, for example, and any referral information that might have happened before this first meeting.

Your job, as the counselor, is to provide support, explore and assess the dynamics of the situation, and simply attempt to engage the person in a way that might ensure the person comes back for a second session. You should use all of the skills you have at your disposal, remembering that *reflections, hunches, and gentle challenges* will most likely be your best working tools. Naturally, you will also be asking some *questions*, but a cautionary: Be judicious in your use of those.

This role play can take approximately 15 minutes, with some time spent afterwards for discussion, review, and feedback. Feedback should be particularly focused on helping the counselor recognize those things that were done that seemed to be particularly helpful.

When all of this is completed, please add your comments about your skills in working with a reluctant client here.

Comments About the Role Play:

_____

_____

_____

_____

And then swap your comments with a peer, or have this reviewed by an instructor.

Peer/Instructor Comments About the Role Play:

_____

_____

_____

_____

Finally, fill out the personal assessment question and comment section that follows. Then swap your assessments with a student colleague or give it to your instructor. This other person can add his thoughts to your assessment, and you may be reviewing his.

Concluding Personal Assessment: Working With a Reluctant Client

Name _____

Which of the following statements best reflects how well you think you understand and will be able to engage a reluctant client? Circle one:

1. I believe that I quite thoroughly understand the necessary skills needed to do this, and I know that I will be able to use them in my work with clients.

2. I understand these skills, but am not sure about how well I'll be able to use them in my counseling work.

3. I'm still pretty unclear about what these skills are all about, and I'm not sure about how to use them.

Comments:

_____

_____

_____

_____

Concluding Peer and/or Instructor Assessment: Working With a Reluctant Client

Which of the following statements best reflects how well you think this person understands and will be able to engage a reluctant client? Circle one:

1. I believe that he/she quite thoroughly understands the necessary skills needed to do this, and I know that he/she will be able to use them in his/her work with clients.

2. I think he/she understands these skills, but I am not sure about how well he/she will be able to use them in his/her counseling work.

3. He/she is still pretty unclear about what these skills are all about, and I'm not sure about how well he/she will be able to use them.

Comments:

_____

_____

_____

_____

12

Putting It
All Together

Using Your Natural and Learned Skills

Introduction

This is the final Skills Practice Session. In this session you will review the natural skills, the motivations, and the beliefs you articulated early on and couple them with the skills you have learned in this course of study. You are also encouraged to think about the impact of what you are learning about counseling theory will have on how you actually do your counseling work. It is this combination of natural and learned skills and your theoretical approach that will define your counseling work.

**DVD
Observation
Reflections**

By now you have most likely watched all of the counseling sessions that were role played on the DVD that accompanies *The Essential Counselor.* If there are any that you haven't viewed, take the time to do that now. Then answer the following:

1. Which of the role plays did you find most compelling? Why?

_____

_____

2. Which, if any, of these counselors on the DVD might you want as a supervisor? Why?

_____

_____

3. All of the skills discussed in this manual were utilized in one way or another in these role plays on the DVD. Do you have any comments/questions about how these were portrayed or used?

_____

_____

REFLECTION EXERCISE: PUTTING IT ALL TOGETHER

In the first chapter of this manual, you were asked to reflect on your beliefs, your life experience, and your natural skills as they will impact the work you do with people. Now that you have additionally put in a considerable amount of effort to gain competency in a new skill set, please take a few minutes to do this reflection again.

Have any of your basic beliefs shifted, or have they remained constant? After receiving considerable feedback from others, do you still see your natural skills in the same way? Are there any significant things that have happened in your life during the time you've been doing this training?

Additionally, reflect on the ways in which you have handled learning the skills that this manual has presented. Do you feel competent to utilize these skills as a counselor?

How has feedback from others regarding your use of these skills affected how you see what you do? What are the things you think you'll need to work on most? What do you feel best about?

If you have already taken, or are taking simultaneously, a course on counseling theory, think about how what you're learning about theory might figure into your actual counseling work.

When you've taken some time to reflect on all of this, write some of your thoughts below:

_____

_____

_____

_____

_____

_____

_____

_____

_____

_____

_____

_____

_____

_____

_____

Role Play: Putting It All Together

You could use the lab practice model outlined in *The Essential Counselor* here, if it seems suitable. Alternatively, you could work with one other student, taking turns as counselor and client, or with a friend or relative if another student is not available. If you are working with observers, their job is to remain silent during the role play, to keep time, and then to provide feedback at the end of the role play.

When you are in the client role (where another student or friend is being the counselor) you will talk about the reflections you've written about—the interplay of your life experiences, your values and beliefs, and your natural and learned helping skills—with the counselor. Talk about your strengths in the things you've learned, and also about where you think you need to concentrate future work. As in the first time you did this, when you talked about your natural helping skills, talk about those things that feel safe. Do not feel compelled to share aspects of your life or beliefs that feel uncomfortable to talk about.

Feel free to also include what you're learning, or have learned, about counseling theory as you discuss your own emerging ideas about yourself as a counselor. How will theory affect how you use these skills, and what other skills will you need to learn in order to effectively utilize the theory or theories that seem to suit you best?

Because you will not have time to discuss all that you've written, you can pick and choose to talk about those things that seem most relevant. Take 20 minutes for this, and then spend 5 minutes talking with the person who served as your counselor about how this went. If there is an observer, that person can also share perspectives on the discussion.

Then the configuration shifts and you switch roles. Allow 20 minutes for each counseling session, with a few minutes of time for feedback.

When you are in the counseling role, try to use as many of the skills that have been introduced in this manual as possible. It may seem a bit artificial to do this, but give it a shot anyway. This skills session is, after all, primarily an opportunity to practice skills. Feel free to use other skills that are discussed in *The Essential Counselor* that have not been reviewed in this Skills Practice Manual.

Again, remember that information that is shared in this, or any, role play should be held confidentially unless there is an explicit understanding that it is ok to talk about it with others. Naturally, if you are concerned about anyone's safety related to information that's been shared, you'll want to discuss that with your instructor. Safety still trumps confidentiality.

When the role plays and discussion of them are completed, list out the skills that you used. If you want, you could rate each one on the one to three scale used in previous skill session reviews. Then make some final comments and reflections in the space provided. As you consider what to write, think about how what you talked about in the client role actually fit, or didn't, with how you operated when you were in the counselor role. Is there congruence between what you actually do and how you think you behave?

When you've finished making comments about the role play, fill out the final personal assessment question and comment section that follows. Then swap your assessments with a student colleague or give it to your instructor. This other person can add their thoughts to your assessment, and you may be reviewing theirs.

Skills Utilized:

_____

_____

_____

_____

Comments About the Role Plays:

_____

_____

_____

_____

Concluding Personal Assessment: Putting It All Together

Name _____

Which of the following statements best reflects how clearly you are able to use your own life experience and beliefs, as well as the skills learned in this course, in your counseling work with others? Circle one:

1. I believe that I quite thoroughly understand my experiences, beliefs, and natural skills—as well as the skills learned in this course—and I know that I will be able to use them together effectively in my work with clients.

2. I have a good understanding of my experiences and beliefs, as well as my natural skills and the skills I've learned in this course, but I am not sure about how well I'll be able to use these in my counseling work.

3. I'm still pretty unclear about what my beliefs and skills are all about, and I'm not sure about how to use them.

Comments:

_____

_____

_____

_____

Concluding Peer and/or Instructor Assessment: Putting It all Together

Which of the following statements best reflects how clearly he/she has articulated and competently demonstrated his/her experiences, beliefs, and natural and learned skills? Circle one:

1. I believe that he/she quite thoroughly understands his/her experiences, beliefs, and skills, and I know that he/she will be able to use them in his/her work with clients.

2. He/she understands these experiences and skills, but I am not sure about how well he/she will be able to use them in his/her counseling work.

3. He/she is still pretty unclear about what his/her beliefs and skills are all about, and I'm not sure how he/she will use them.

Comments:

_____

_____

_____

_____

Reviewer Name _____

About the Author

 **Dr. Hutchinson** did his undergraduate work at the University of Vermont, received his Master of Arts in Counseling from Assumption College, and his doctorate from the State University of New York at Buffalo.

He has worked as an addictions counselor, as an administrator of treatment programs, and as a private counseling practitioner. He has also driven taxis, moved furniture, and been a houseparent for teens.

David Hutchinson now prepares both undergraduate and graduate students for careers in psychology and counseling at Johnson State College in Vermont. His areas of special focus are foundation skills training, group work, addictions, and grief counseling.

A former Peace Corps Volunteer in Jamaica, David's priorities includes travel and maintaining an international perspective in his life and work. He's trained counselors in Grenada, and he's established sister school relationships between five schools in Vermont and Grenada. In the fall of 2010, he orchestrated a professional counselor exchange between the country of St. Kitts/Nevis and the state of Vermont.

He regularly takes groups of students to Nicaragua to give his students an opportunity to learn the unique ways the indigenous people of the region deal with addiction and mental illness. In Vermont, David continues his emphasis on intensive, process-oriented coursework with long weekend retreats at an off-campus lodge near Caspian Lake in the woods of Vermont's Northeast Kingdom.

In 2006, David was honored with the Distinguished Faculty of the Year Award at Johnson State College. He holds positions on the boards of the New England Institute of Addiction Studies and local mental health and service organizations.

He lives in St. Albans, Vermont, with his wife, Katharine. They have two grown children.